*P*rogressive
Cross-Stitch

Progressive
Cross-Stitch

Fast to Fantastic Variations from Single Patterns

By Terrece Beesley

Sterling Publishing Co., Inc. New York

A Sterling/Chapelle Book

For Chapelle Limited

Owner: Jo Packham

Editor: Amanda McPeck

Staff: Malissa Boatwright, Sara Casperson, Rebecca Christensen, Amber Hanson, Cherie Hanson, Holly Hollingsworth, Susan Jorgensen, Susan Laws, Barbara Milburn, Leslie Ridenour, Cindy Rooks, Cindy Stoeckl, Kelly Valentine-Cracas, Ryanne Webster, Nancy Whitley and Lorrie Young.

Ribbon Embroidery: Mary Jo Hiney

Photography: Kevin Dilley of Hazen Photography

Library of Congress Cataloging-in-Publication Data

Beesley, Terrece.
Progressive cross-stitch : fast to fantastic variations from single patterns / by Terrece Beesley.
p. cm.
"A Sterling/Chapelle book."
Includes index.
ISBN 0-8069-3181-7
1. Cross-stitch--Patterns. 2. Silk ribbon embroidery.   I. Title
TT778.C76.B44 1995   95-15641
746.44'3041--dc20   CIP

1 3 5 7 9 10 8 6 4 2

Published by Sterling Publishing Company, Inc.
387 Park Avenue South, New York, N.Y. 10016
© 1995 by Chapelle Limited
Distributed in Canada by Sterling Publishing
c/o Canadian Manda Group, One Atlantic Avenue, Suite 105
Toronto, Ontario, Canada M6K 3E7
Distributed in Great Britain and Europe by Cassell PLC
Wellington House, 125 Strand, London WC2R 0BB, England
Distributed in Australia by Capricorn Link (Australia) Pty Ltd.
P.O. Box 6651, Baulkham Hills, Business Centre, NSW 2153, Australia
Printed and Bound in Hong Kong

Sterling ISBN 0-8069-3181-7

Welcome to Progressive Cross-Stitch!

To make this "Progressive Cross-Stitch" book, *Terrece Beesley* has taken small motifs and added to them to make progressively larger and more intricate designs. The result is a wonderful collection of "all-in-one" cross-stitch designs–from **fast** to *fantastic*! You can stop stitching at any point in the design or finish the entire design to make an heirloom piece. Or you can work all of the stages separately for a perfectly coordinating decor for your home.

Each graph is color-coded by stage. The color of the stage is indicated by the color of the number preceding the sample information for that stage. For instance, Stage 1 of "A Rabbit in the Garden" is purple. So, the purple section of the graph is Stage 1. In most cases, the next stage will include all previous stages. Therefore, if you want to stitch Stage 2 of "A Rabbit in the Garden," you will stitch both the purple and pink parts of the graph. Where the graph for a stage is different from preceding or following pages, we have included a separate graph.

For several pieces, we have included ideas of how to incorporate ribbon embroidery in the designs. A full-color diagram shows you where you can embellish your finished cross-stitch piece or replace part of the cross-stitched designs with ribbon flowers. General instructions and ribbon stitch instructions are included at the end of the book, starting on page 132.

Contents

A Rabbit in the Garden

1

Stitched on cream Cashel linen 28 over 2 threads, the finished design size is 1⅞" x 2⅛". The fabric was cut 9" x 9".

Fabrics	Design Sizes
Aida 11	2½" x 2⅝"
Aida 18	1½" x 1⅝"
Hardanger 22	1¼" x 1⅜"

Stitch Count: 27 x 29

2

Stitched on cream Cashel linen 28 over 2 threads, the finished design size is 5⅛" x 5⅝". The fabric was cut 9" x 10".

Fabrics	Design Sizes
Aida 11	6½" x 7⅛"
Aida 18	4" x 4⅜"
Hardanger 22	3¼" x 3½"

Stitch Count: 71 x 78

3

Stitched on cream Cashel linen 28 over 2 threads, the finished design size is 8¼" x 6¼". The fabric was cut 14" x 14".

Fabrics	Design Sizes
Aida 11	10½" x 8"
Aida 18	6⅜" x 4⅞"
Hardanger 22	5¼" x 4"

Stitch Count: 115 x 88

4

Stitched on cream Cashel linen 28 over 2 threads, the finished design size is 13⅝" x 8¼". The fabric was cut 19" x 14".

Fabrics	Design Sizes
Aida 11	17¼" x 10½"
Aida 18	10½"" x 6½"
Hardanger 22	8⅝" x 5¼"

Stitch Count: 190 x 116

5

Stitched on cream Cashel linen 28 over 2 threads, the finished design size is 13⅜" x 8¾". The fabric was cut 19" x 14".

Fabrics	Design Sizes
Aida 11	17" x 11⅛"
Aida 18	10⅜" x 6¾"
Hardanger 22	8½" x 5½"

Stitch Count: 187 x 122

6

Stitched on cream Cashel linen 28 over 2 threads, the finished design size is 15⅞" x 12⅜". The fabric was cut 22" x 19".

Fabrics	Design Sizes
Aida 11	20⅛" x 15⅞"
Aida 18	12⅜" x 9⅝"
Hardanger 22	10⅛" x 7⅞"

Stitch Count: 222 x 174

Anchor   DMC (used for sample)

Step 1: Cross-stitch (2 strands)

Anchor		DMC	
1	– ╱		White
300	·	745	Yellow-lt. pale
891	✚	676	Old Gold-lt.
4146	U ╱U	754	Peach-lt.
8	+	353	Peach
6	K	3824	Apricot-lt.
328	N	3341	Apricot
11	◆	351	Coral
10	◒	3712	Salmon-med.
25	○	3326	Rose-lt.
31	♥	3708	Melon-lt.
26	↔	894	Carnation-vy. lt.
76	B	962	Wild Rose-med.
42	◑	335	Rose
104	⁒	210	Lavender-med.
98	☐	553	Violet-med.
101	W	327	Antique Violet-vy. dk.
119	▲	333	Blue Violet-dk.
215	G	320	Pistachio Green-med.
876	■	502	Blue Green
264	⌐	772	Pine Green-lt.
266	✳	471	Avocado Green-vy. lt.
267	M	469	Avocado Green
242	◇	989	Forest Green
244	∴	987	Forest Green-dk.
858	Z	524	Fern Green-vy. lt.
859	✕	522	Fern Green
862	✿	3362	Pine Green-dk.
376	J ╱J	842	Beige Brown-vy. lt.
378	★ ╱·	841	Beige Brown-lt.
347	△	402	Mahogany-vy. lt.
338	E	3776	Mahogany-lt.
349	✱	301	Mahogany-med.
360	♠ ╱·	898	Coffee Brown-vy. dk.
397	H ╱H	453	Shell Gray-lt.
399	●	451	Shell Gray-dk.
300	╱	⌐ 745	Yellow-lt. pale
4146		╲ 754	Peach-lt.
266	S	⌐ 471	Avocado Green-vy. lt.
347		╲ 402	Mahogany-vy. lt.
242	R	⌐ 989	Forest Green
338		╲ 3776	Mahogany-lt.
244	◪	⌐ 987	Forest Green-dk.
349		╲ 301	Mahogany-med.

Step 2: Backstitch (1 strand)

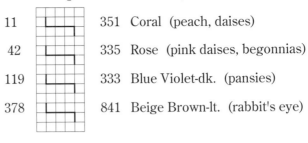

11		351	Coral (peach, daises)
42		335	Rose (pink daises, begonnias)
119		333	Blue Violet-dk. (pansies)
378		841	Beige Brown-lt. (rabbit's eye)

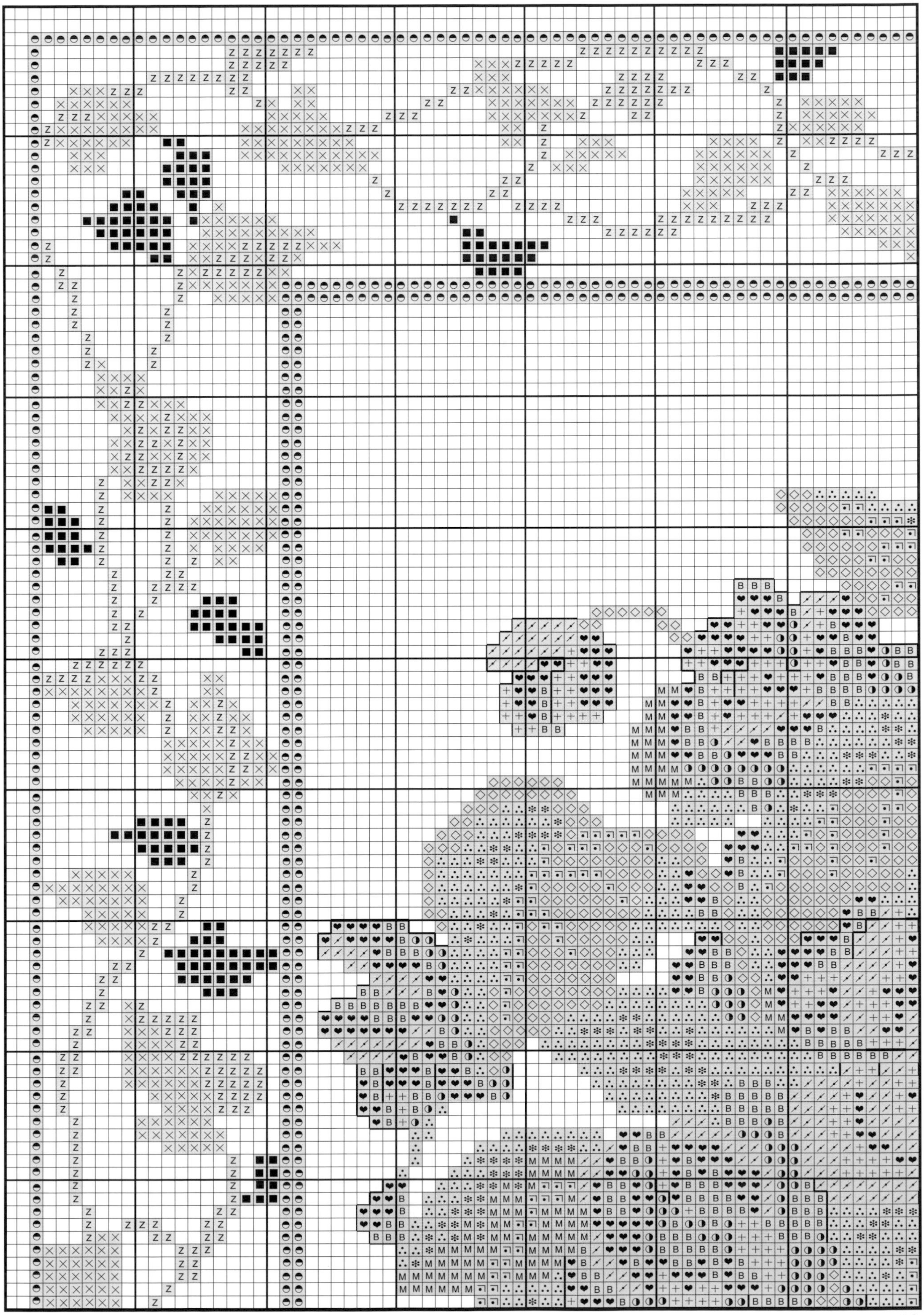

All Stages, Top Center Left

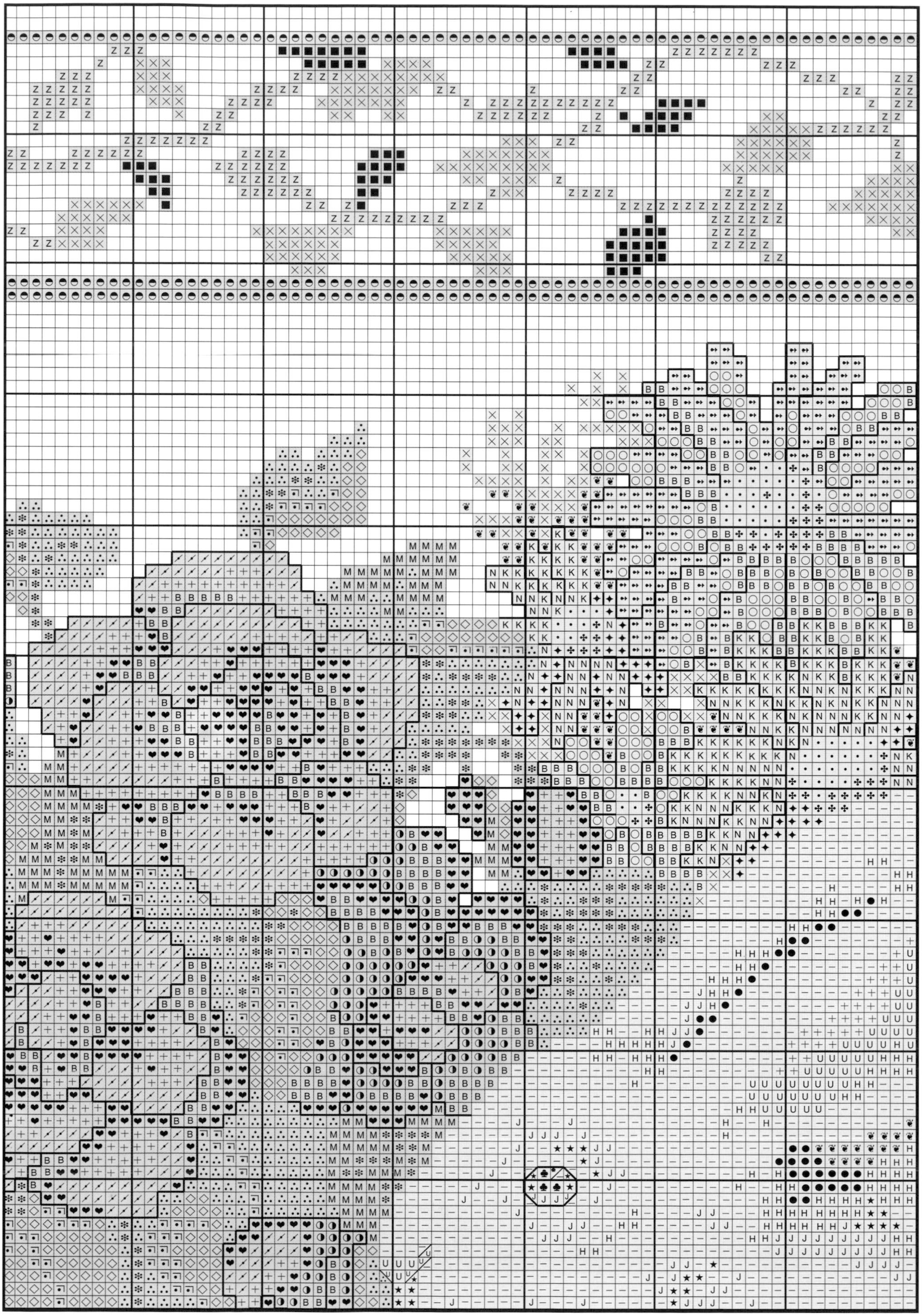

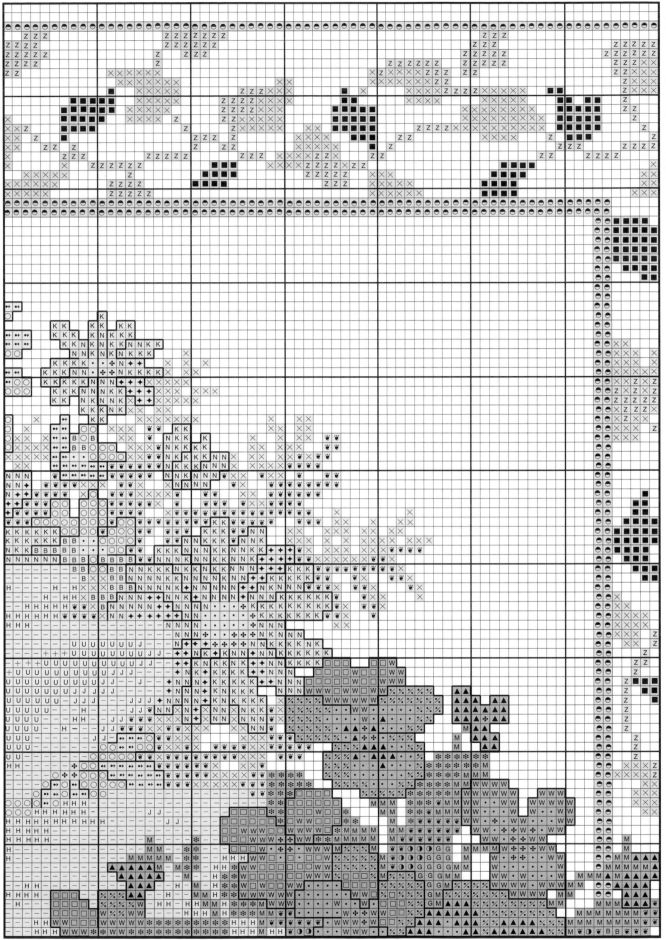

To the Daisy

Bright Flower! whose home is everywhere,
Bold in maternal Nature's care,
And all the long year through the heir
Of joy and sorrow;
Methinks that there abides in thee
Some concord with humanity,
Given to no other flower to see
The forest through!

Is it that Man is soon deprest?
A thoughtless Thing! who, once unblest,
Does little on his memory rest,
Or on his reason,
And Thou wouldst teach him how to find
A shelter under every wind,
A hope for times that are unkind
And every season?

Thou wander'st the wide world about,
Unchecked by pride or scrupulous doubt
With friends to greet thee, or without,
Yet pleased and willing;
Meek, yielding to the occasion's call,
And all things suffering from all,
They function apostolical
In peace fulfilling.

William Wordsworth

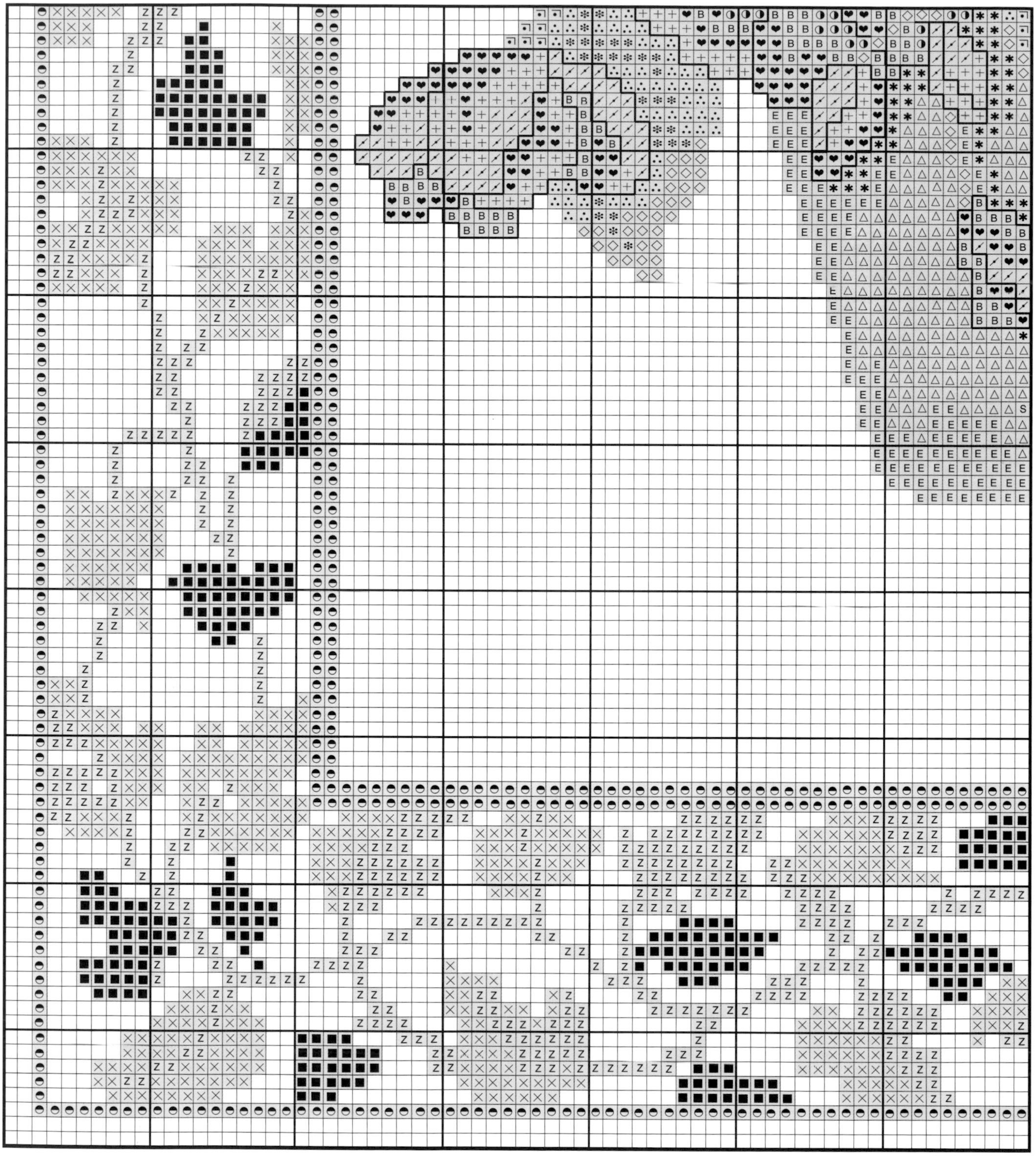

All Stages, Bottom Left

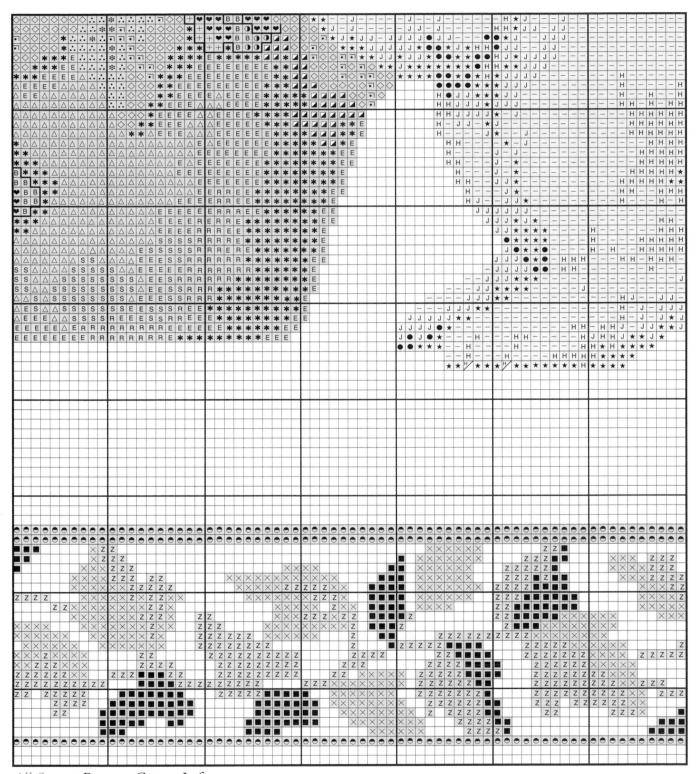

All Stages, **Bottom Center Left**

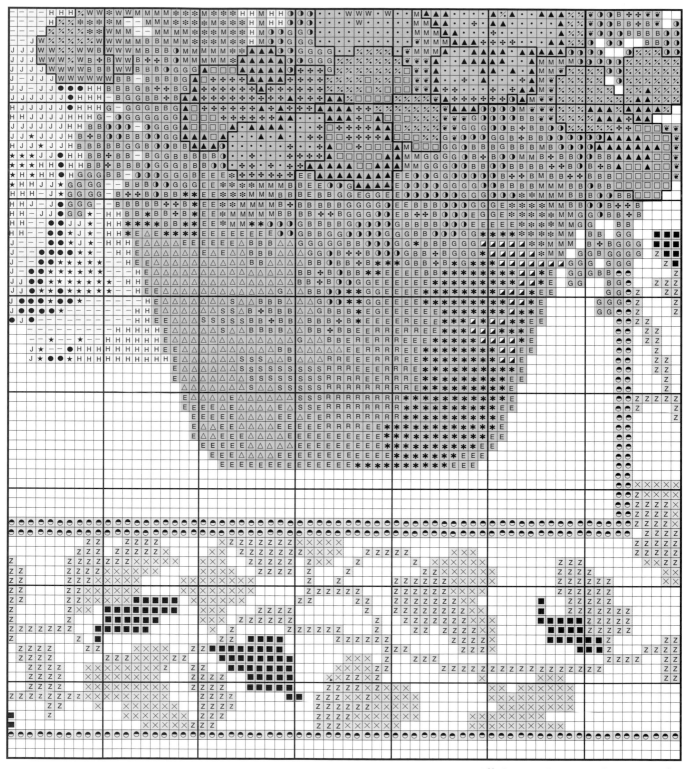

All Stages, Bottom Center Right

All Stages, Bottom Right

A Thing of Beauty

A thing of beauty is a joy for ever:
Its loveliness increases; it will never
Pass into nothingness; but still will keep
A bower quiet for us, and a sleep
Full of sweet dreams, and health, and quiet
breathing.
Therefore, on every morrow, are we wreathing
A flowery band to bind us to the earth,
Spite of despondence, of the inhuman dearth
Of noble natures, of the gloomy days, Of all
the unhealthy and o'er-darkened ways
Made for our searching: yes, in spite of all,
Some shape of beauty moves away the pall
From our dark spirits.

John Keats

3-Journal Cover

Materials

Completed cross-stitch
Purchased journal 6¼" x 8 ½"
   or larger
12" ecru moiré
12" fleece
⅝ yard matching trim
2 yards matching satin cording
1 yard coordinating ½"
   ribbon
Poster board
Tacky glue
Spray adhesive
Hot glue gun and glue sticks
Masking tape

Directions

1

From poster board, cut two pieces that fit the measurements of the inside cover of book. Cut one oval shape that your cross-stitch piece will cover and also fit on the front of the book.

2

Cut ecru moiré into the following pieces: one rectangle, 2" larger on all sides than the book when it is open, and two pieces, 1" larger on all sides than poster board panels. From fleece, cut one oval shape and one rectangle the same size as the book when opened.

3

Trim stitched cross-stitch 1" larger than the oval cardboard piece. With spray adhesive, glue fleece to one side of cardboard oval. Stretch cross-stitch over fleece and hot-glue edges onto the back. Glue the decorative trim onto the underside of oval so that the edging shows on the front. Cut a piece of satin cording to fit around the oval and glue into place around the outside edge.

4

Cover the two poster board panels with material, using spray adhesive and stretching tightly and taping the extra fabric onto the back. Set aside.

5

With spray adhesive, attach the fleece to the front and back cover of the book. Trim as necessary.

6

Lay book down in the center of the wrong side of the moiré. Starting at the bottom, cut two slits in the material, on both sides of the binding, until you get to the book edge. Tuck this piece of fabric into the book binding and glue into place. Repeat with top edge.

7

Cut corner sections of fabric off, leaving about ½" to cover corners. Starting at the center, tacky-glue fabric to inside of book, pulling snugly as you go. (It helps if you close your book slightly to avoid getting the cover too tight.) Glue the top and bottom first and then the corners and side edges.

8

Cut the ribbon in half and glue one end to center edge of inside cover. Repeat with other half of ribbon on back cover.

9

Hot-glue the two fabric-covered panels onto the inside front and back cover. Glue satin cording around edges of these panels for a finished look.

10

With hot glue, attach your cross-stitch oval to front of book, holding down firmly until glue cools. Tie book closed with ribbon.

1-Porcelain Jar Materials

Completed cross-stitch
Pale yellow mounting
   needlework porcelain jar
4mm silk ribbon: dark green
   and light green
Seed beads: mauve and gold

Directions

1

Mount cross-stitch on porcelain jar, following manufacturer's directions.

2

Randomly stitch ribbon stitches around cross-stitch for leaves (see page 137).

3

Randomly sew beads in top left corner of cross-stitch. (See page 133.)

4-Keepsake Box Materials

Completed cross-stitch
Wooden box with lid: 7½" x
   15½" x 10"
8¼" x 13" piece of cardboard
8¼" x 13" fleece
1¼ yards ivory braid
Masking tape
Hot glue gun and glue sticks

Directions

1

Trim cross-stitch 2" larger on each side than cardboard. Glue fleece to top of cardboard. Center cross-stitch over fleeces and tape onto back. After piece is in place, staple edges, stretching tightly. Place masking tape over unfinished edges.

2

Glue braid to box top ½" from edge. Mount cross-stitch on top of braid and box lid with hot glue.

5-Pillow Materials

Completed cross-stitch
   trimmed to 16½" x 12"
⅝ yard lavender moiré
½ yard pink moiré
½ yard muslin
Matching thread
12 oz. bag of stuffing

Directions
(All seams ¼".)

1

Cut two pieces of pink moiré 19"x 14½" and two pieces of lavender moiré 22" x 17½". Place pink moiré right sides together and sew a seam around edge, leaving an opening to turn. Clip corners, turn and press. Whipstitch opening closed. Repeat with lavender moiré.

2

Zigzag the edges of the stitched piece. Turn edges under ½" and press.

3

Cut two pieces of muslin 16¼" x 11½" and stitch around edges, leaving an opening to turn. Turn and stuff firmly. Stitch opening closed.

4

Layer and center materials in the following order: lavender moiré, pink moiré and stitched piece. Pin in place. Machine-stitch around inside edge of stitched piece through all thicknesses, leaving one side open. Place muslin pillow between lavender and pink moiré and pin opening closed before stitching.

Diagram reduced 50 %.

Symbol	Stitch	Color	Amt.	Size	Type
	Geranium Bud	Pink	22"	⅝"	Wired
	2 and 3 Petal Pansy	Ivory	22"	⅜"	Web
	Ribbon Stitch	Dark Pink	36"	4mm	Silk
	Pistil Stitch	Mauve Brown	18"	4mm	Silk
	Top Butterfly wing	Yellow/Green	6"	1"	Wired
	Bottom Butterfly wing	Orange/Green	5"	1"	Wired

Symbol	Stitch	Color	Amt.	Size	Type
	Pansy	Pink/Green	18"	⅝"	Wired
	Pansy	Purple/Pink	36"	1"	Wired
	French Knot (3)	Yellow	72"	4mm	Silk
	Wild Rose	Dark Pink	18"	7mm	Silk
	Wild Rose	Light Pink	55"	7mm	Silk
	Ribbon Stitch	Dark Green	55"	7mm	Silk
	Jonquil Leaves	Olive Green	9"	½"	Wired

Diagram reduced 75 %.

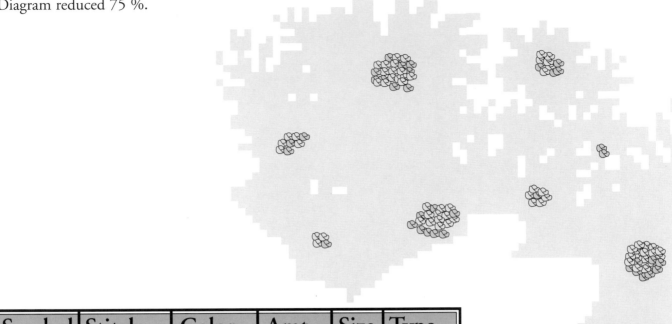

Symbol	Stitch	Color	Amt.	Size	Type
✿	French Knot	Yellow	72"	4mm	Silk
✿	French Knot	Golden Brown	72"	4mm	Silk

Diagram reduced 90 %.

Angel of the Nursery

1

Stitched on white Cashel linen 28 over 2 threads, the finished design size is 4" x 3½". The fabric was cut 8" x 8".

Fabrics	Design Sizes
Aida 11	5" x 4½"
Aida 18	3" x 2¾"
Hardanger 22	2½" x 2¼"

Stitch Count: 55 x 49

2

Stitched on white Cashel linen 28 over 2 threads, the finished design size is 6" x 5⅜". The fabric was cut 9" x 9".

Fabrics	Design Sizes
Aida 11	7⅝" x 6⅞"
Aida 18	4⅝" x 4⅛"
Hardanger 22	3⅞" x 3⅜"

Stitch Count: 84 x 75

3

Stitched on white Cashel linen 28 over 2 threads, the finished design size is 6⅜" x 9⅞". The fabric was cut 8" x 12".

Fabrics	Design Sizes
Aida 11	8⅛" x 12⅝"
Aida 18	5" x 7¾"
Hardanger 22	4" x 6⅜"

Stitch Count: 89 x 139

4

Stitched on white Cashel linen 28 over 2 threads, the finished design size is 6⅜" x 13¼". The fabric was cut 13" x 20".

Fabrics	Design Sizes
Aida 11	8⅛" x 16⅞"
Aida 18	5" x 10¼"
Hardanger 22	4⅛" x 8⅜"

Stitch Count: 90 x 185

Anchor   DMC (used for sample)

Step 1: Cross-stitch (2 strands)

Anchor		DMC	
1	·		White
386	+ /	746	Off White
301	○	744	Yellow-pale
891	×	676	Old Gold-lt.
890	♣	729	Old Gold-med.
373	◑	3045	Yellow Beige-dk.
366	↔	951	Peach Pecan-lt.
4146	z /z	754	Peach-lt.
892	B	225	Shell Pink-vy. lt.
49	△	963	Wild Rose-vy. lt.
49	✳	3689	Mauve-lt.
66	●	3688	Mauve-med.
8	★ /	761	Salmon-lt.
868	G /G	758	Terra Cotta-lt.
914	U /	3064	Pecan-lt.
975	□ /	3753	Antique Blue-vy. lt.
920	♥ /	932	Antique Blue-lt.
214	/	368	Pistachio Green-lt.
216	▲	367	Pistachio Green-dk.
379	∴ /	840	Beige Brown-med.
380	■ /	839	Beige Brown-dk.

Step 2: Backstitch (1 strand)

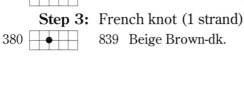

890	729	Old Gold-med. (off-white and peach flowers)
66	3688	Mauve-med. (pink flowers, cradle, name)
920	932	Antique Blue-lt. (angel's dress, baby's clothing)
380	839	Beige Brown-dk. (hands, face of angel, rabbit, bear, baby's hair)

Step 3: French knot (1 strand)

380	●	839	Beige Brown-dk.

Stage 2, Left

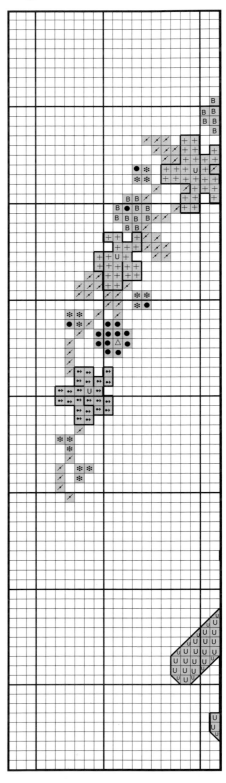

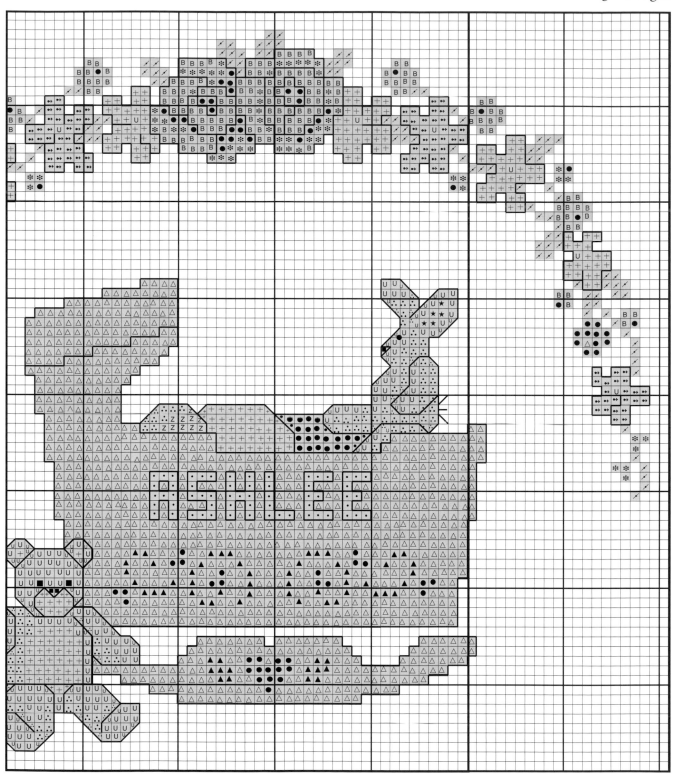

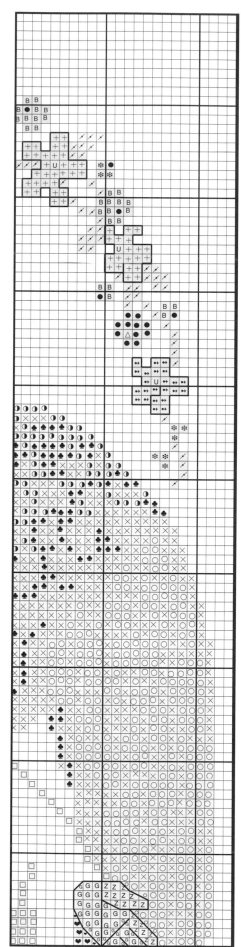

Stages 1, 3, and 4, Top Right

Stages 1, 3, and 4, Bottom Left

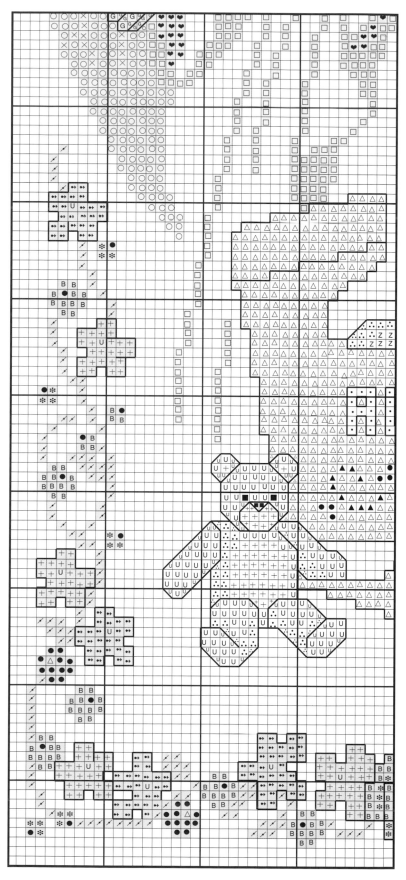

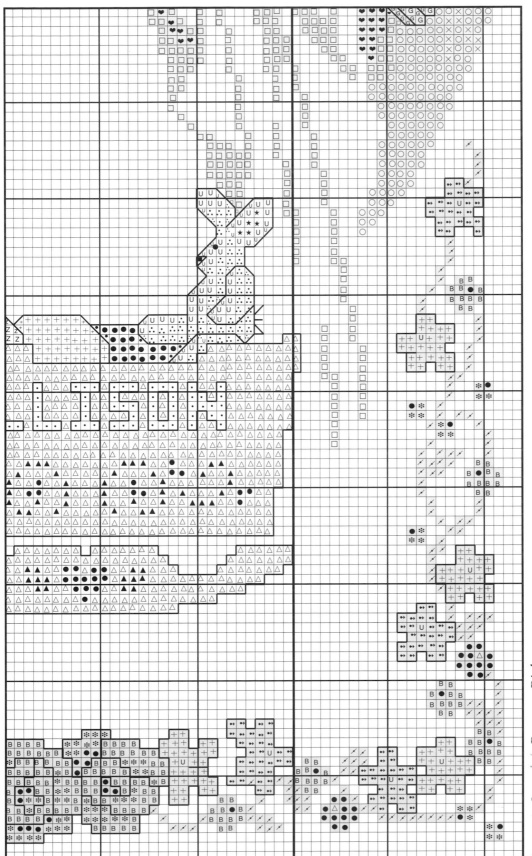

Stages 1, 3, and 4, Bottom Right

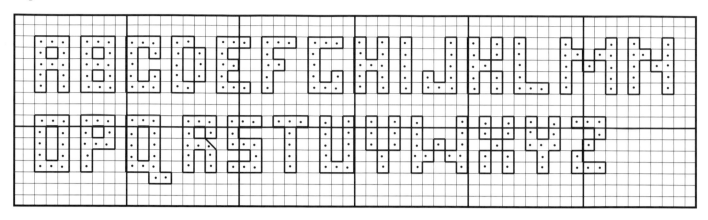

1-Keepsake Box Materials

Completed cross-stitch
Mounting needlework box 6¼"
    square and 2½" deep
Fleece square to fit in lid top
    opening
Matching cording to fit around
    opening on lid top
Country blue acrylic paint
Glue

Directions

1

Paint box country blue.

2

Following manufacturer's
instructions, trim cross-stitch
and mount using fleece for
cushion.

3

Glue cording around edge of
cross-stitch to finish.

2-Pillow Materials

Completed cross-stitch trimmed to 9" x 9"
14" pillow form
Two 15" squares of pink satin; matching thread
12" Battenburg doily; matching thread
2 yards matching piping
Small amount of stuffing

Directions

1

Layer and center in the following order: pink satin square, stitched piece and doily; pin in place. Hand-baste in circle around stitching through all layers.

2

With scissors, trim away excess white Aida cloth from under doily. Satin-stitch around circle. Trim away center of doily so that cross-stitch shows through. Satin-stitch again around this edge.

3

Turn pillow front over and make a small slit in satin underneath center of cross-stitch . Stuff lightly and whipstitch closed. This will raise your cross-stitch up above pillow.

4

Sew piping around front of pillow ½" in from edge. Place other satin square face down onto pillow front and sew around edges along outside of piping, leaving an opening to turn. Clip curves, turn and insert pillow form. Whipstitch opening closed.

3-Photo Album Materials

Completed cross-stitch
1 yard light blue polished cotton
½ yard small lace trim
2 yards each of three 4mm silk ribbon
Bear charm
½ yard fleece
Photo album
Poster board
Glue gun and glue sticks
Spray adhesive
Marking pencil

Directions

1

Cut two poster board pieces to fit inside measurement of album cover. Using spray adhesive, attach fabric to poster board. Set aside.

2

Using spray adhesive, attach fleece to outside cover of album, front and back.

3

Cut one 18" x 45" piece of blue fabric. Place stitched piece and blue fabric right sides together and stitch together on left side. Wrap around album to get measurement and placement. Pin, mark, and trim excess fabric, allowing 1½" extra on all sides for gluing.

4

Start gluing front cover first. Pull snugly as you go. Keep book in semiclosed position for best fit. Mark center of binding of book on both sides at each end. Clip fabric up to binding; tuck flap into binding and glue. Finish gluing to cover. Glue inside flaps in place.

5

Slip ribbons through back of book and tie bow at top. Tie bear charm onto end of ribbon and add love knots.

Symbol	Stitch	Color	Amt.	Size	Type	Special Instructions
	Ribbon Stitch	Dark Pink	54" in all	4mm	Silk	
	Ribbon Stitch	Medium Pink	70" in all	4mm	Silk	
	Ribbon Stitch	Light Pink	72" in all	4mm	Silk	
	Spider Web Rose	3 shades of Pink	see above	4mm	Silk	Dark center, medium middle, light outer
	Lazy Daisy	Pale Yellow	72"	4mm	Silk	5 for each flower
	Lazy Daisy	Pale Tan	50"	4mm	Silk	5 for each flower
	French Knot (2)	Golden Brown	24"	4mm	Silk	
	Lazy Daisy	Bright Green	57" in all	4mm	Silk	Tuck leaves under previous stitches
	Ribbon Stitch	Bright Green	see above	4mm	Silk	
	1-twist Ribbon Stitch	Bright Green	see above	4mm	Silk	
	Lazy Daisy	Dark Pink	see above	4mm	Silk	
	Cascade	Light Pink	see above	4mm	Silk	

Charms
"Baby"
Heart
Rose
Rocking Horse

"Baby" Charm

Rose Charm

Heart Charm

Rocking Horse Charm

To Every Season

1

Stitched on cream Murano linen 30 over 2 threads, the finished design size is 1⅜" x 1⅜". The fabric was cut 6" x 6".

Fabrics	Design Sizes
Aida 11	1⅞" x 1⅞"
Aida 14	1⅜" x 1⅜"
Aida 18	1⅛" x 1⅛"
Hardanger 22	⅞" x ⅞"

Stitch Count: 20 x 20

2

Stitched on light mocha Cashel linen 28 over 2 threads, the finished design size is 7¾" x 2". The fabric was cut 14" x 6".

Fabrics	Design Sizes
Aida 11	9⅞" x 2½"
Aida 18	6" x 1½"
Hardanger 22	5" x 1¼"

Stitch Count: 109 x 28

3

Stitched on pewter Murano 30 over 2 threads, the finished design size is 5⅝" x 5⅝". The fabric was cut 10" x 10".

Fabrics	Design Sizes
Aida 11	7⅝" x 7⅝"
Aida 14	6" x 6"
Aida 18	4⅝" x 4⅝"
Hardanger 22	3⅞" x 3⅞"

Stitch Count: 84 x 84

4

Stitched on white Murano 30 over 2 threads, the finished design size is 7½" x 5⅝". The fabric was cut 8" x 10".

Fabrics	Design Sizes
Aida 11	10⅛" x 7⅝"
Aida 14	8" x 6"
Aida 18	6¼" x 4⅝"
Hardanger 22	5⅛" x 3⅞"

Stitch Count: 112 x 84

5

Stitched on white Cashel linen 28 over 2 threads, the finished design size is 8" x 11¼". The fabric was cut 14" x 18".

Fabrics	Design Sizes
Aida 11	10⅛" x 14⅜"
Aida 18	6¼" x 8¾"
Hardanger 22	5⅛" x 7⅛"

Stitch Count: 112 x 158

Anchor **DMC (used for sample)**

Step 1: Cross-stitch (2 strands)

Anchor		DMC (used for sample)
1	· / ⁄.	White
386	◇ / ◒	3823 Yellow-ultra pale
301	z / z	744 Yellow-pale
305	◑ / ◔	3822 Straw-lt.
306	★ / ⁄.	3820 Straw-dk.
323	G	722 Orange Spice-lt.
62	S	3806 Cyclamen Pink-lt.
42	●	309 Rose-deep
158	✐	775 Baby Blue-vy. lt.
130	N	809 Delft
177	+ / ⁄+	3807 Cornflower Blue
149	✢ / ⁄✢	336 Navy Blue
186	♥	959 Seagreen-med.
264	△	772 Pine Green-lt.
203	⬔	954 Nile Green
210	×	562 Jade-med.
212	∴	561 Jade-vy. dk.
337	○	3778 Terra Cotta
936	◆ / ⁄.	632 Pecan-dk.
386	M	3823 Yellow-ultra pale
158		775 Baby Blue-vy. lt.
130	♠	809 Delft
212		561 Jade-vy. dk.

Step 2: Backstitch (1 strand)

Anchor		DMC
177		3807 Cornflower Blue (mountains, snowline)
149		336 Navy Blue (sun/moon, lettering and seagull)
936		632 Pecan-dk. (2 strands, everything else)

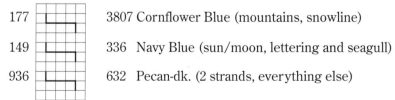

Stage 2, Left

Stage 2, Right

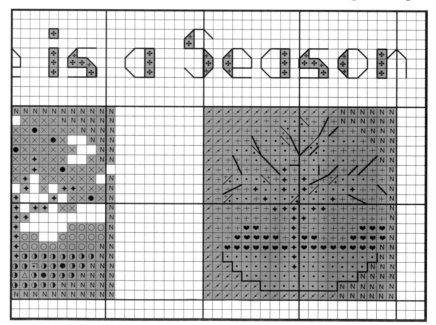

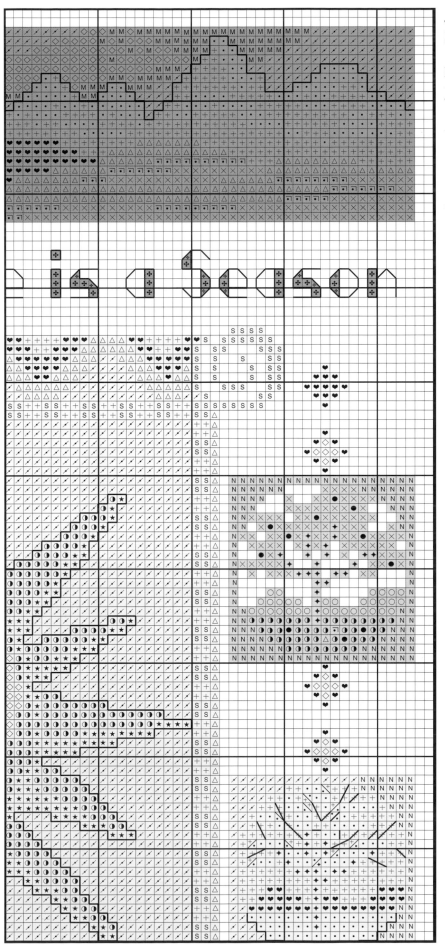

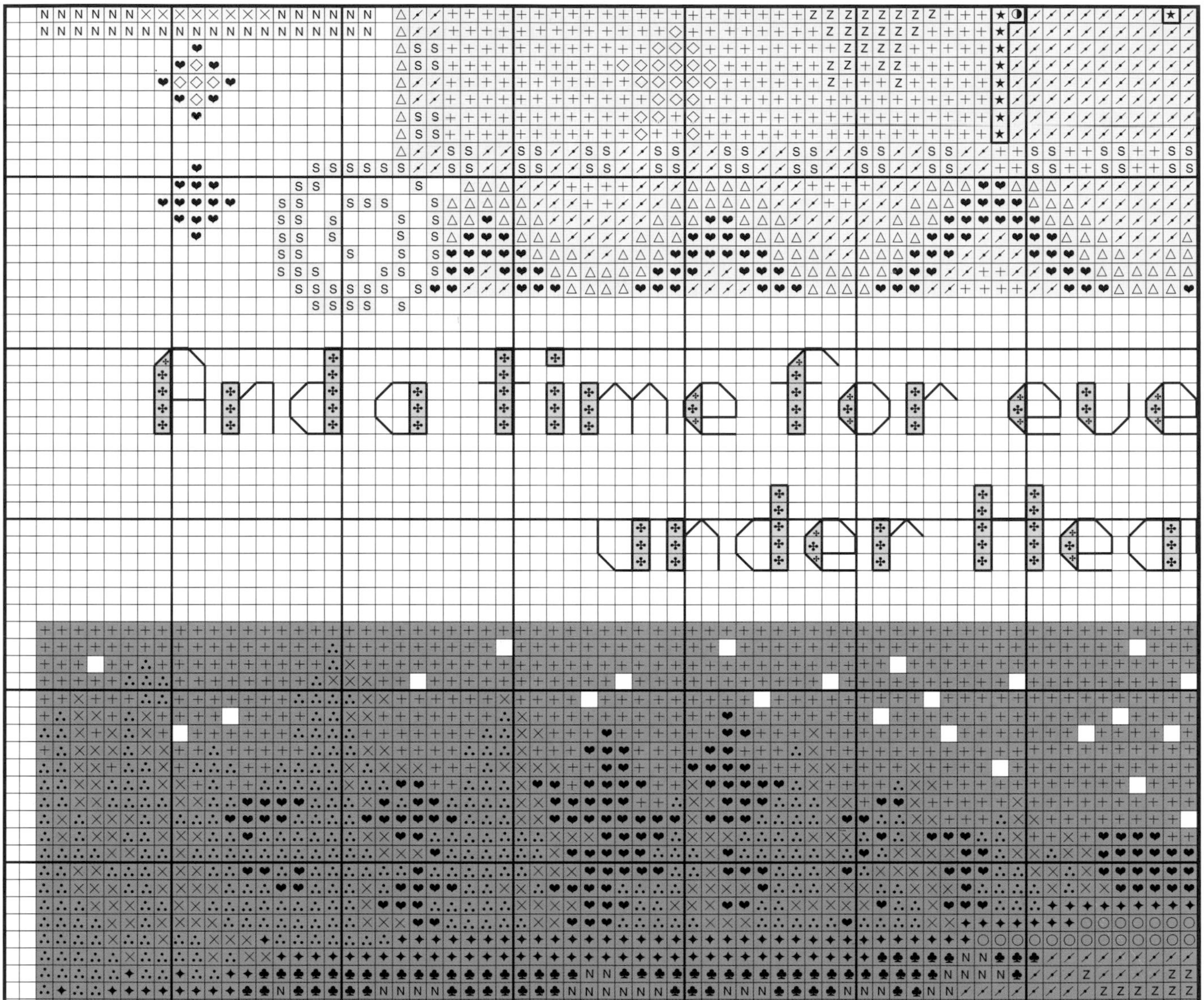

Stages 1, 3, 4, and 5, Bottom Left

1-Lamp Pull Materials

Completed cross-stitch
Two 1¼" squares of cardboard
Small scrap of wool
5" length of ¼" jute
24" of narrow twine for hanging
3 assorted wood beads
Spray adhesive
Tacky glue

Directions

1

With spray adhesive, mount completed cross-stitch on one square of cardboard. Wrap edges around back and secure with tacky glue. Trim wool to fit on other cardboard square and mount in the same manner.

2

Thread beads onto the twine, going back up through first and second bead again. Pull twine until ends are even and then tie a knot. Spread glue onto wrong sides of cardboard pieces. Slide beads to the bottom of the twine and then position this between the cardboard squares.

3

Trim jute to fit around the edges of the square and glue into place. Note: A little glue on the ends of the jute will prevent unraveling while you are attaching.

3-Footstool Materials

Completed cross-stitch
Needlework mounting footstool: 8"x 8"x 6"
Two fleece squares to fit top measurement of stool
1 yard navy wool yarn
1 yard ⅜"-wide jute
Navy blue acrylic paint
Paintbrush

Directions

1

Remove top piece from footstool. Sand stool and paint navy blue. Let dry.

2

Trim the completed cross-stitch 2" larger all around than the top section of the footstool. Stitch a frame around cross-stitch with navy blue yarn. Mount completed piece over two layers of fleece onto the top section of the footstool.

3

If footstool has holes on the sides for handles, cut a piece of jute and knot one end. Feed through holes and knot other end. Repeat with other side. If the box does not have holes, drill a small hole on each side using a ¼" bit, or omit this step.

4

Fit mounted cross-stitch into the top and secure.

4-Pillow Materials

Completed cross-stitch
¼ yard navy blue wool
¼ yard hunter green wool
½ yard light brown wool
Matching thread
Wool yarn: hunter green and
   navy blue
Stuffing

Directions

1

Trim cross-stitch to 7" x 9". Cut a 7" x 9" block from each of the wool fabrics. Stitch cross-stitch and navy blue wool together on one side. Press open. Stitch hunter green and light brown wool together in same manner. Press. Pin top of hunter green/light brown strip to bottom of cross-stitch/navy blue strip, making sure that the blocks line up evenly. Sew together and press.

2

With navy blue yarn, cross-stitch the left and bottom edges of the navy blue block, overlapping onto connecting blocks. With hunter green yarn, blanket-stitch the top and right edges of the hunter green block, overlapping as before.

3

From light brown wool, cut a pillow back to match size of front. Place front and back, right sides together, and sew around sides, leaving a 6" opening. Clip corners, turn and stuff firmly. Whipstitch opening closed.

---

from **The Sun Rising**

Busy old fool, unruly sun,
Why dost thou this,
Through windows, and through curtains call on us?
Must to thy motions lover's seasons run?
Saucy pedantic wretch, go chide
Late school-boys, and sour prentices,
Go tell court-huntsmen that the King will ride,
Call country ants to harvest offices;
Love, all alike, no season knows, nor clime,
Nor hours, days, months, which are the rags of time.

John Donne

2-Pillow Materials

Completed cross-stitch
½ yard light brown wool
⅛ yard each; navy blue and
hunter green wool
2 yards hunter green wool yarn
Matching thread for
construction
Stuffing

Directions

1

Centering cross-stitch , trim the cross-stitched piece to 12"x 3½". From navy blue and hunter green wool, cut eight triangles using pattern on page 56. From light brown wool, cut two 12"x 4" strips, two 16"x 4" strips and one 18"x 16" piece.

2

Starting with the triangles, sew a navy blue and a hunter green piece together to form a square. Press seam open. Repeat with remaining triangles. Sew four squares together to make a strip the same size as the cross-stitch. Repeat with remaining squares. Press seams. Sew one strip to the top of the cross-stitch and one strip to the bottom of the cross-stitch. Press.

3

With the 12"x 4" strips of light brown wool, sew one to the top of the navy blue/hunter green squares and one to the bottom. Sew the last two pieces of light brown wool to each side of the cross-stitch . With yarn, baste a border about ½" outside cross-stitch edge. Trim the pillow back to the same measurement as the pillow front.

4

Place pillow back and front, right sides together, and sew around edges, leaving an opening for stuffing. Clip corners, turn and stuff firmly. Whipstitch opening closed.

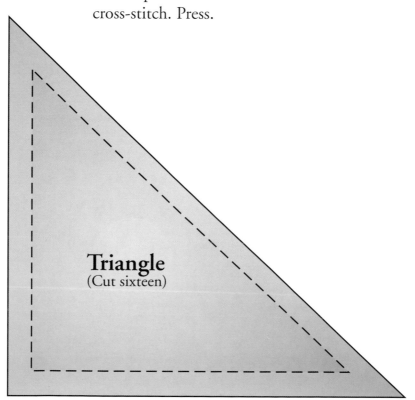

Triangle
(Cut sixteen)

To every thing there is a season, and a time to every purpose under the heaven:

a time to be born, and a time to die;

a time to plant, and a time to pluck up that which is planted;

a time to kill, and a time to heal;

a time to break down, and a time to build up;

a time to weep, and a time to laugh;

a time to mourn, and a time to dance;

a time to cast away stones, and a time to gather stones together;

a time to embrace and a time to refrain from embracing;

a time to get, and a time to lose;

a time to keep, and a time to cast away;

a time to rend, and a time to sew;

a time to keep silence, and a time to speak;

a time to love, and a time to hate, a time of war, and a time of peace.

Ecclesiastes 3:1-8

Noah's Ark

1

Stitched on buttercup Meran 28 over 2 threads, the finished design size is 7⅝" x 2⅝". The fabric was cut 14" x 6".

Fabrics	Design Sizes
Aida 11	9⅝" x 3¼"
Aida 18	5⅞" x 2"
Hardanger 22	4⅞" x 1⅝"

Stitch Count: 106 x 36

2

Stitched on white Lugano linen 25 over 2 threads, the finished design size is 8¾" x 7⅛". The fabric was cut 12" x 10".

Fabrics	Design Sizes
Aida 11	10" x 8⅛"
Aida 14	7⅞" x 6⅜"
Aida 18	6⅛" x 5"
Hardanger 22	5" x 4"

Stitch Count: 110 x 89

3

Stitched on white Lugano linen 25 over 2 threads, the finished design size is 10¼" x 8¾". The fabric was cut 17" x 15".

Fabrics	Design Sizes
Aida 11	11⅝" x 9⅞"
Aida 14	9⅛" x 7 3/4"
Aida 18	7⅛" x 6"
Hardanger 22	5⅞" x 5"

Stitch Count: 128 x 109

Anchor   **DMC (used for sample)**

Step 1: Cross-stitch (2 strands)

Anchor			DMC	
1				White
303			742	Tangerine-lt.
330			947	Brunt Orange
46			666	Christmas Red-bright
88			718	Plum
975			3753	Antique Blue-vy. lt.
920			932	Antique Blue-lt.
130			809	Delft
131			798	Delft-dk.
133			796	Royal Blue-dk.
238			703	Chartreuse
203			564	Jade-vy. lt.
210			562	Jade-med.
309			435	Brown-vy. lt.
371			433	Brown-med.
890			3827	Golden Brown-pale
884			3826	Golden Brown
351			400	Mahogany-dk.
382			3371	Black Brown

Step 2: Backstitch (1 strand)

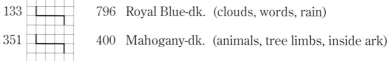

Anchor		DMC	
133		796	Royal Blue-dk. (clouds, words, rain)
351		400	Mahogany-dk. (animals, tree limbs, inside ark)
382		3371	Black Brown (around ark)

Step 3: French knot (1 strand)

382		3371	Black Brown

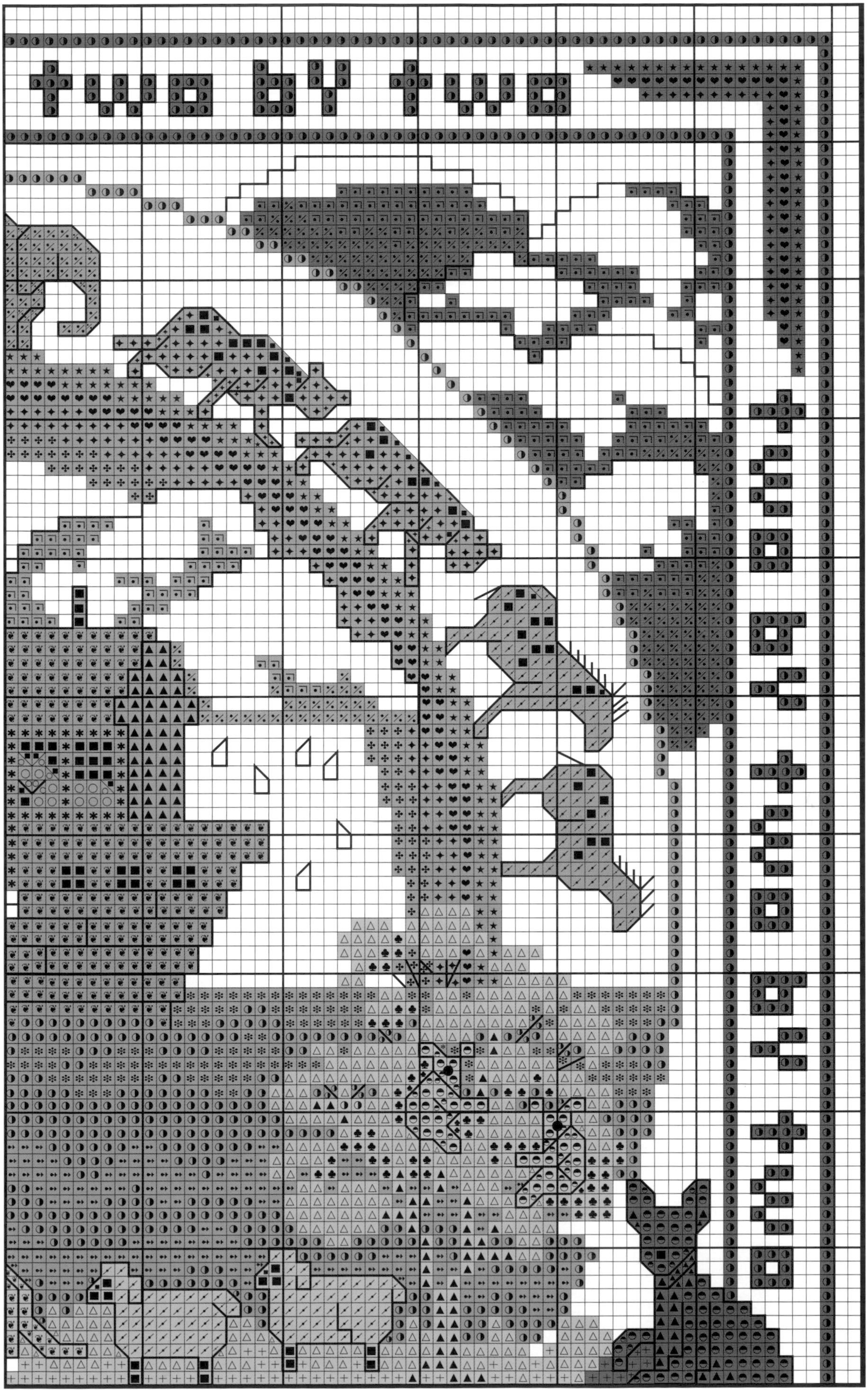

Stages 1, 2, and 3, Top Right

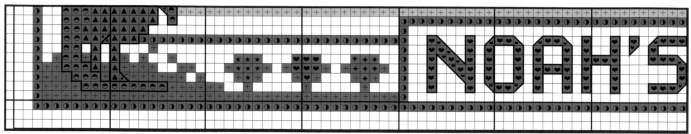

Stages 1, 2, and 3, Bottom Left

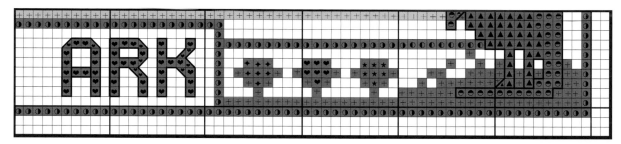

Stages 1, 2, and 3, Bottom Right

2-Keepsake Box Materials

Completed cross-stitch
Wooden box with lid (ours is hinged and measures 12"x 10" x 9")
¼" plywood cut to fit top of box
Double thickness of fleece cut to fit top of box
1¼ yard red cording
Acrylic paint: red and navy blue
Paintbrush
Sandpaper
Masking tape
Hot glue gun and glue sticks

Directions

1

Sand box and paint navy blue with red trim. Let dry.

2

Trim cross-stitch 2" larger all around than plywood. Glue double fleece to top of plywood. Place cross-stitch piece over fleece and tape onto back. After piece is in place, staple edges, stretching tightly. Place masking tape over unfinished edges and mount to top of box lid with hot glue.

Cat in a Window

1

Stitched on peach Lugano 25 over 2 threads, the finished design size is 2½" x 2¼". The fabric was cut 8" x 8".

Fabrics	Design Sizes
Aida 11	3" x 2½"
Aida 14	2¼" x 2"
Aida 18	1¾" x 1½"
Hardanger 22	1½" x 1¼"

Stitch Count: 32 x 28

2

Stitched on cream Murano 30 over 2 threads, the finished design size is 6" x 3¼". The fabric was cut 10" x 8".

Fabrics	Design Sizes
Aida 11	8⅛" x 4½"
Aida 14	6⅜" x 3½"
Aida 18	5" x 2 3/4"
Hardanger 22	4⅛" x 2¼"

Stitch Count: 90 x 49

3

Stitched on light mocha Cashel linen 28 over 2 threads, the finished design size is 6" x 5¾". The fabric was cut 14" x 12".

Fabrics	Design Sizes
Aida 11	8⅛" x 7⅞"
Aida 14	6⅜" x 6⅛"
Aida 18	5" x 4¾"
Hardanger 22	4⅛" x 3⅞"

Stitch Count: 90 x 86

4

The overlay is stitched on Poly-silk 30 over 2 threads, the finished design size is 7½" x 10⅝". The fabric was cut 14" x 17". The background is stitched on amaretto Murano 30 over 2 threads, the finished design size is 6" x 5¾". The fabric was cut 14" x 17".

Background

Fabrics	Design Sizes
Aida 11	8⅛" x 7⅞"
Aida 14	6⅜" x 6 1/8"
Aida 18	5" x 4¾"
Hardanger 22	4⅛" x 3⅞"

Stitch Count: 90 x 86

Overlay

Fabrics	Design Sizes
Aida 11	10¼" x 14½"
Aida 14	8½" x 11⅜"
Aida 18	6¼" x 8⅞"
Hardanger 22	5⅛" x 7¼"

Stitch Count: 113 x 159

Cat

Overlay

Anchor			DMC (used for sample)

Step 1: Cross-stitch (2 strands)

Anchor			DMC (used for sample)
1	+	⊿	White
868	▽		758 Terra Cotta-lt.
337	✛		3778 Terra Cotta
5975	●		356 Terra Cotta-med.
914	▲		3064 Pecan-lt.
11	✳	✳	351 Coral
13	◆	⊿	349 Coral-dk.
47	♥		304 Christmas Red-med.
24	⅘		776 Pink-med.
75	□	⊿	3733 Dusty Rose-lt.
76	★	⊿	3731 Dusty Rose-med.
920	⬓	⊿	932 Antique Blue-lt.
121	▼		793 Cornflower Blue-med.
95	◠◠	⊿	554 Violet-lt.
110	◖		209 Lavender-vy. dk.
214	╱	⊿	368 Pistachio Green-lt.
216	♣		367 Pistachio Green-dk.
265	∴		3348 Yellow Green-lt.
843	×		3364 Pine Green
861	◔	⊿	3363 Pine Green-med.
246	■		895 Christmas Green-dk.
890	◇	⊿	3827 Golden Brown-pale
307	◑	⊿	977 Golden Brown-lt .
884	✳	✳	3826 Golden Brown
355	◢		975 Golden Brown-dk.

Step 2: Backstitch (1 strand)

355		975 Golden Brown-dk. (cat)
76		3731 Dusty Rose-med. (tulips)
121		793 Cornflower Blue-med. (bottles, floor)

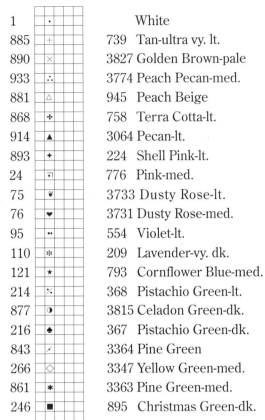

Step 1: Cross-stitch (2 strands)

Anchor		DMC (used for sample)
1	·	White
885	+	739 Tan-ultra vy. lt.
890	×	3827 Golden Brown-pale
933	∴	3774 Peach Pecan-med.
881	△	945 Peach Beige
868	✛	758 Terra Cotta-lt.
914	▲	3064 Pecan-lt.
893	◆	224 Shell Pink-lt.
24	⬓	776 Pink-med.
75	✦	3733 Dusty Rose-lt.
76	♥	3731 Dusty Rose-med.
95	◠◠	554 Violet-lt.
110	✳	209 Lavender-vy. dk.
121	★	793 Cornflower Blue-med.
214	⅘	368 Pistachio Green-lt.
877	◖	3815 Celadon Green-dk.
216	♣	367 Pistachio Green-dk.
843	╱	3364 Pine Green
266	◇	3347 Yellow Green-med.
861	✳	3363 Pine Green-med.
246	■	895 Christmas Green-dk.

Step 2: Backstitch (1 strand)

76		3731 Dusty Rose-med. (flowers)

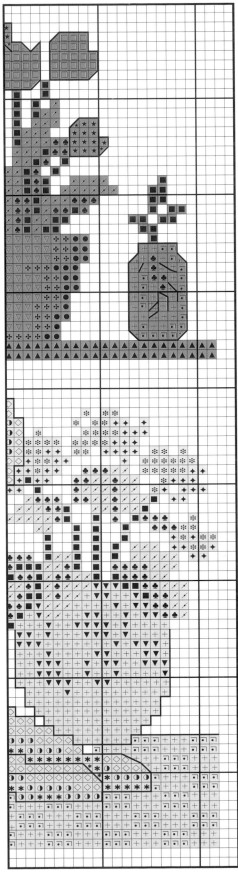

The Tyger

Tyger, Tyger, burning bright
In the forests of the night;
What immortal hand or eye,
Could frame thy fearful symmetry?

In what distant deeps or skies
Burnt the fire of thine eyes!
On what wings dare he aspire?
What the hand, dare seize the fire?

And what shoulder, and what art,
Could twist the sinews of thy heart?
And when thy heart began to beat,
What dread hand? and what dread feet?

What the hammer? what the chain?
In what furnace was thy brain?
What the anvil? what the dread grasp
Dare its deadly terrors clasp?

When the stars threw down their spears
And water'd heaven with their tears:
Did he smile his work to see?
Did he who made the Lamb make thee?

Tyger, Tyger, burning bright
In the forest of the night:
What immortal hand or eye,
Could frame thy fearful symmetry?

William Blake

Stage 4 (Overlay), Top Left

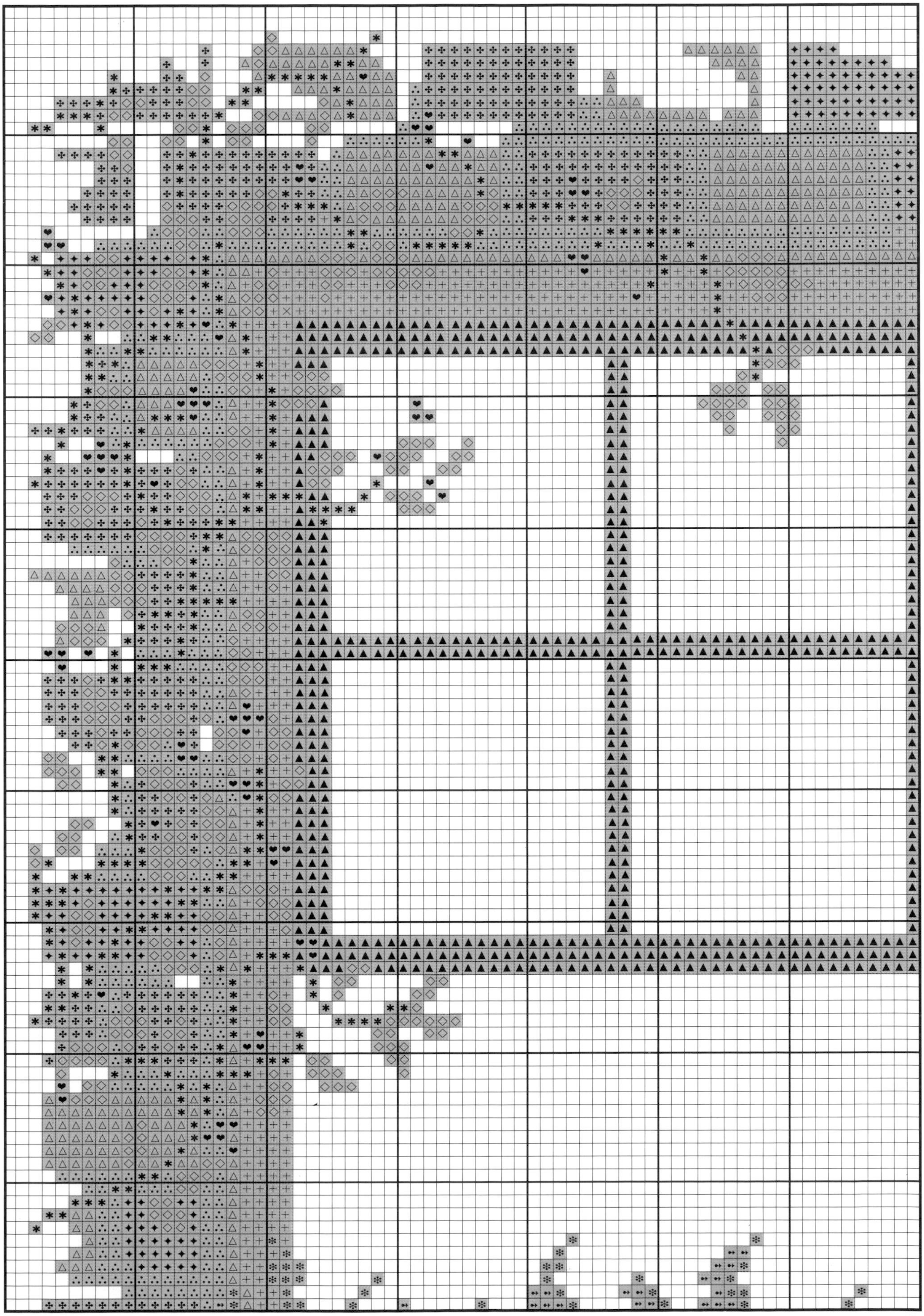

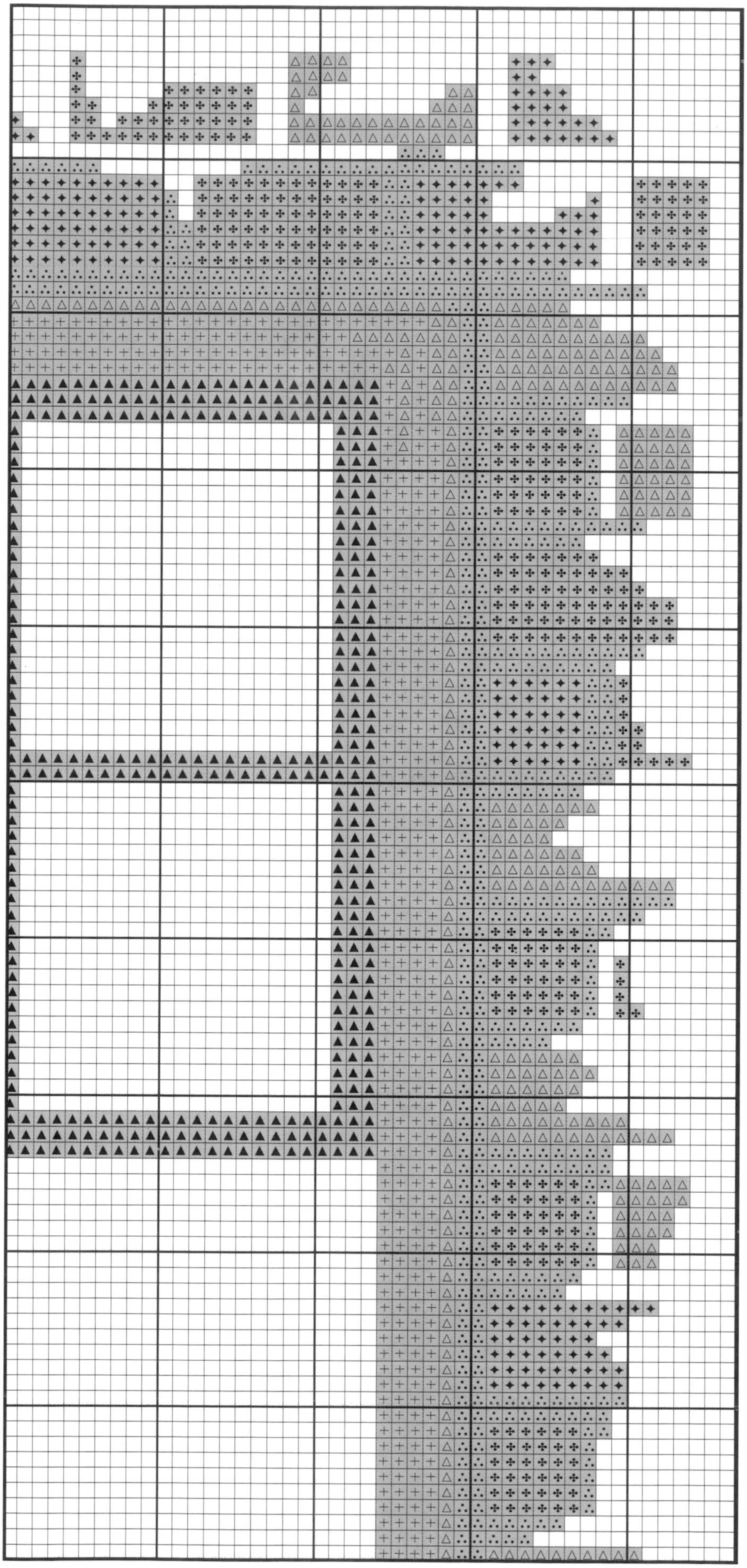

Stage 4 (Overlay), Top Right

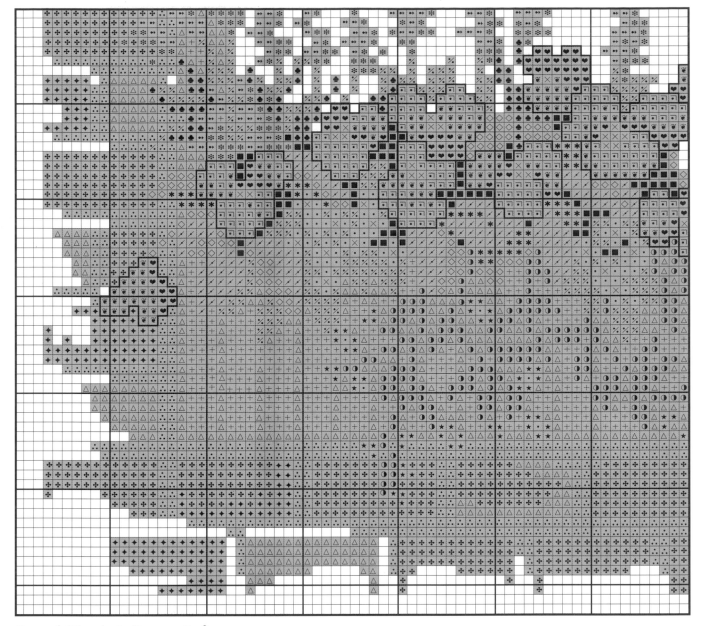

Stage 4 (Overlay), Bottom Left

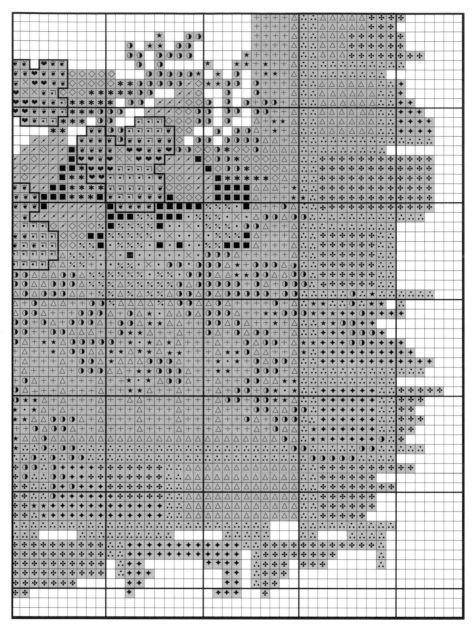

Stage 4 (Overlay), Bottom Right

1-Sachet
Materials

Completed cross-stitch
    trimmed to 4½" x 4"
Coordinating fabric cut
    4½" x 4"
Two fleece rectangles cut
    4½" x 4"
16" of tatting or lace trim
9" of matching cording
Potpourri

Directions

1

Layer materials in the following manner: fleece, desired fragrance, fleece, coordinating fabric, face up; stitched piece, face down. Stitch around edges through all thicknesses, leaving top open to turn. Clip corners, turn and press. Insert cording between sachet in top center. Whipstitch opening closed.

2

Hand-sew trim around edge of sachet.

3-Frame
Materials

Completed framed cross-stitch
9" square white cotton fabric
¼" checkerboard craft stencil
Brown paint or stain
Light blue paint
1 popsicle or craft stick
Stencil brush
Fray preventative
Glue

Directions

1

Stencil checker print onto white fabric with the blue paint to match cross-stitch. Apply fray preventative on raw edges.

2

Cut in half diagonally. Fold two corners under so that it fits the tablecloth in stitched piece. Hand-tack to picture and let fabric flow over frame.

3

Cut the popsicle stick in half and paint brown. When dry, glue sticks ½" from edge of tablecloth, creating legs.

Bee Charm

Cat Charm

80

Symbol	Stitch	Color	Amt.	Size	Type
	French Knot	White	32"	4mm	Silk
	French Knot	Yellow	12"	4mm	Silk
	1-twist Ribbon Stitch	Pale Green	29"	4mm	Silk
	1-twist Ribbon Stitch	Olive Green	29"	4mm	Silk
	Lazy Daisy	Lavender	12" in all	4mm	Silk
	Ribbon Stitch	Red	18"	4mm	Silk
	Ribbon Stitch	Bright Pink	18"	4mm	Silk
	Ribbon Stitch	Dusty Rose	18"	4mm	Silk
	1-twist Ribbon Stitch	Dark Green	18" in all	4mm	Silk
	1-twist Ribbon Stitch	Medium Green	46"	4mm	Silk
	1-twist Ribbon Stitch	Light Green	54"	4mm	Silk
	French Knot (2)	Dark Peach	46" in all	4mm	Silk
	Lazy Daisy	Dark Green	see above	4mm	Silk
	Ribbon Stitch	Dark Peach	see above	4mm	Silk
	French Knot (2)	Light Peach	48"	4mm	Silk
	1-twist Ribbon Stitch	Lavender	see above	4mm	Silk

Charms
Bee
Cat

A heart
filled with Love
always has
something
to give.

Love Is All Around

1

Stitched on waste canvas 14 over 2 threads, the finished design size is 2" x 2⅜". The canvas was cut 5" x 5".

Fabrics	Design Sizes
Aida 11	2½" x 3"
Aida 14	2" x 2⅜"
Aida 18	1½" x 1⅞"
Hardanger 22	1¼" x 1¼"

Stitch Count: 28 x 33

2

Stitched on white cashel linen 28 over 2 threads, the finished design size is 5¼" x 4¼". The fabric was cut 12" x 12".

Fabrics	Design Sizes
Aida 11	6⅝" x 5⅝"
Aida 14	5¼" x 4½"
Aida 18	4" x 3½"
Hardanger 22	3⅜" x 2⅞"

Stitch Count: 73 x 62

3

Stitched on ash rose Lugano 25 over 2 threads, the finished design size is 6⅞" x 6⅞". The fabric was cut 14" x 14".

Fabrics	Design Sizes
Aida 11	7⅞" x 7⅞"
Aida 14	6⅛" x 6⅛"
Aida 18	4¾" x 4¾"
Hardanger 22	3⅞" x 3⅞"

Stitch Count: 86 x 86

84

4

Stitched on ash rose Lugano 25 over 2 threads, the finished design size is 9⅛" x 10½". The fabric was cut 16" x 17".

Fabrics	Design Sizes
Aida 11	10⅜" x 12"
Aida 14	8⅛" x 9⅜"
Aida 18	6⅜" x 7⅜"
Hardanger 22	5⅛" x 6"

Stitch Count: 114 x 132

Anchor **DMC (used for sample)**

Step 1: Cross-stitch (2 strands)

Anchor		DMC	
1			White
48		818	Baby Pink
24		776	Pink-med.
27		899	Rose-med.
26		957	Geranium-pale
76		961	Wild Rose-dk.
8		353	Peach
10		352	Coral-lt.
104		210	Lavender-med.
158		775	Baby Blue-vy. lt.
128		800	Delft-pale
130		799	Delft-med.
214		368	Pistachio Green-lt.
210		562	Jade-med.
885		739	Tan-ultra vy. lt.

Step 2: Backstitch (1 strand)

Anchor	DMC	
24	776	Pink-med. (border)
27	899	Rose-med. (large white flowers)
76	961	Wild Rose-dk. (lettering)
130	799	Delft-med. (large blue bow)

Step 3: French knot (1 strand)

Anchor	DMC	
76	961	Wild Rose-dk.

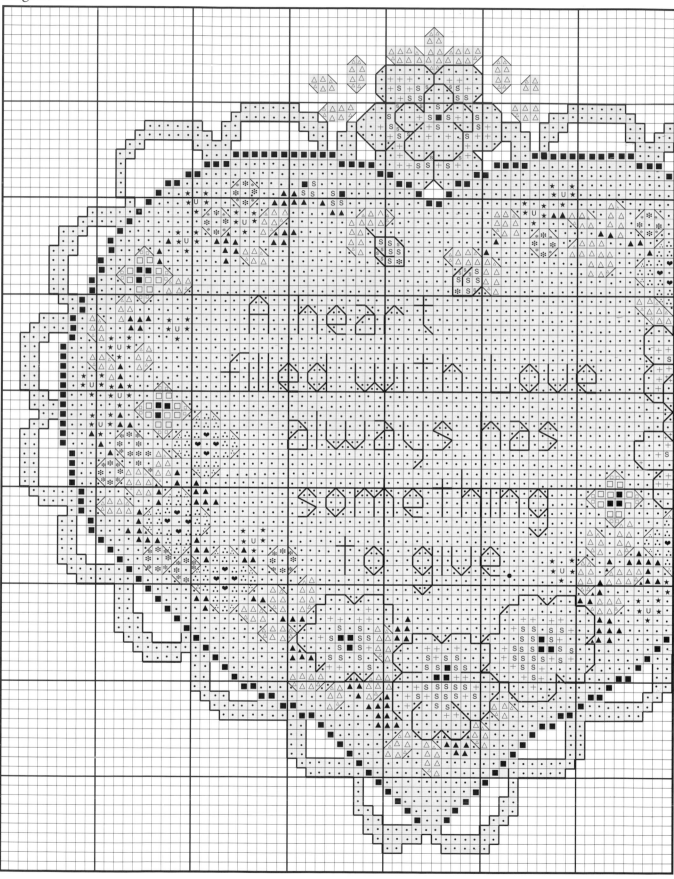

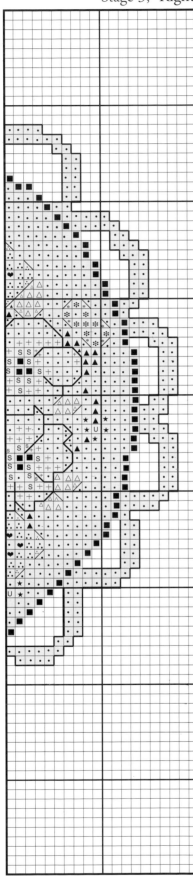

Sonnet XXIX

When, in disgrace with fortune and men's eyes,
I all alone beweep my outcast state,
And trouble deaf heaven with my bootless cries,
And look upon myself and curse my fate,
Wishing me like to one more rich in hope,
Featured like him, like him with friends possessed,
Desiring this man's art, and that man's scope,
With what I most enjoy contented least;
Yet in these thoughts myself almost despising,
Haply I think on thee, and then my state,
Like to the lark at break of day arising
From sullen earth, sings hymns at heaven's gate;
For thy sweet love remembered such wealth brings,
That then I scorn to change my state with kings.

William Shakespeare

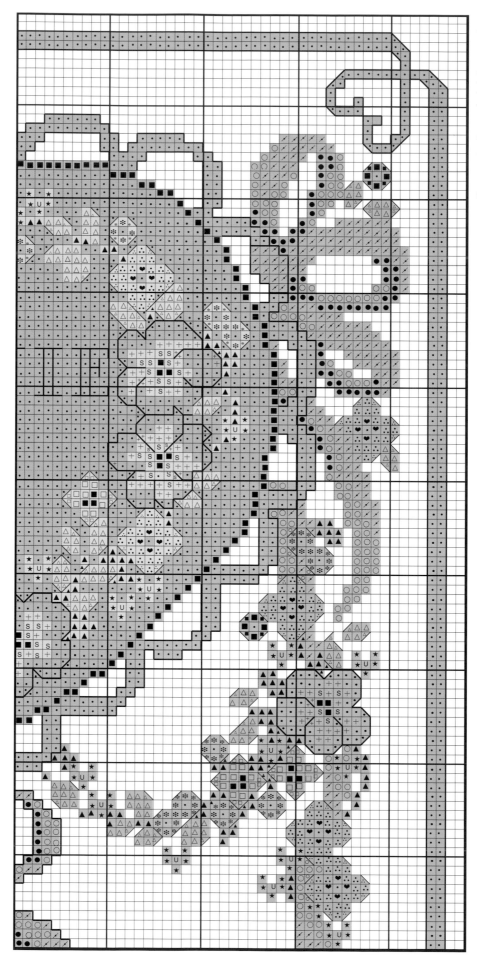

Stages 1, 2, and 4, Bottom Left

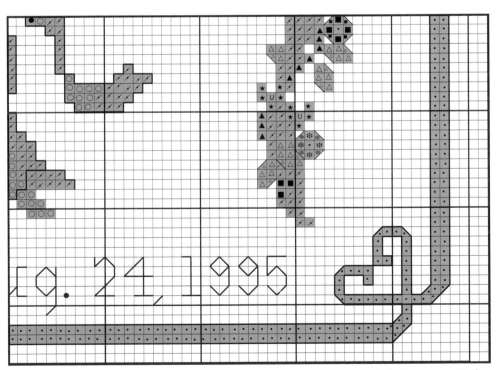

Stages 1, 2, and 4, Bottom Right

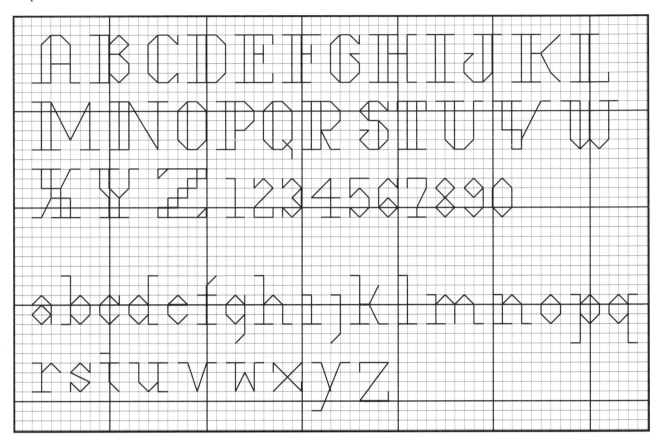

1-Rice Bag Materials

Completed cross-stitch; see
    Step 2
1/8 yard white velvet
12" Three inch-wide white
    fringe
24" white cording
Light blue thread
Light blue dye

Directions

1

Dye velvet, fringe and cording
with dye according to
manufacturer's instructions.
Let dry.

2

Cut velvet into two 6" x 7"
pieces. Zigzag all raw edges.
Attach a 4" x 4" piece of 14-
count waste canvas in the
center of one velvet piece.
Stitch cross-stitch and remove
waste canvas, following
manufacturer's instructions.

3

Place both velvet pieces right
sides together. Pin fringe edge
inside bottom edge so that the
fringe lays inside. Starting at
the top of one side, stitch
around bag until you get 1"
from the top of other side.
Leave 1/2" opening and stitch
last 1/2" closed. Turn.

4

Fold top edge under 1/2" to
form a casing for the cording.
Sew. Thread cording through
casing with safety pin and then
knot ends of cord. Fray ends
and trim even.

2-Ring Pillow Materials

Completed cross-stitch
¼ yard white bridal satin; matching thread
2½ yards 6"-wide lace
1¼ yard each: pink, lavender and peach 4mm silk ribbon
1 yard pearl trim with bias edge
Cherub charm
Stuffing

Directions

1

Fold lace in half and miter point. Trim away excess. Baste around edge of lace and pull thread to gather. Set aside. (You may use pregathered lace if you prefer.)

2

Enlarge heart pattern on page ninety-five 150 %. From pattern, cut one heart from satin and one using the finished cross-stitch.

3

Using your zipper foot, baste pearl trim around front edges of cross-stitch heart, pearls facing in. Pin ruffle into place, matching points, with the right side facing pillow top. Baste ruffle. (The ruffle will be all bunched together, but after pillow is turned, it will fall nicely around edge.)

4

Pin satin back on the front of pillow, making sure that all lace stays inside. Sew around edge, leaving a 4" opening. Clip curves and turn. Stuff pillow firmly and whipstitch opening closed.

5

Handling the three lengths of silk ribbon as one, tie a bow in the middle and tack to center of pillow. Tie a cherub into one of the tails.

3-Victorian Pillow Materials

Completed cross-stitch trimmed to 12½" square
12" pillow form
½ yard white moiré; matching thread
15" square muslin
15" square fleece
48" of decorative white rose trim
Eight 2" white tassels

Directions
(All seams ¼".)

1

From white moiré, cut two strips 15½" x 2¼" and two strips 12½" x 2¼". Starting with the shorter strips, sew one to the top and one to the bottom of the cross-stitch piece. Sew the longer strips onto the sides. Using triangle pattern on page 95, cut off corners of square. Using octagon shape as a pattern, cut squares from white moiré, muslin and fleece.

2

Layer cross-stitch piece, fleece and muslin and pin together. Hand-baste rose trim around cross-stitch inset, making sure to go through all layers. Pin pillow front and remaining white moiré right sides together and clip off corners. Stitch around three sides and turn.

3

Going through all layers, hand-baste along the same line as rose trim on same three sides. Insert pillow form in pocket and finish stitching. Whipstitch outer opening closed. Tack tassels to each point on the corners.

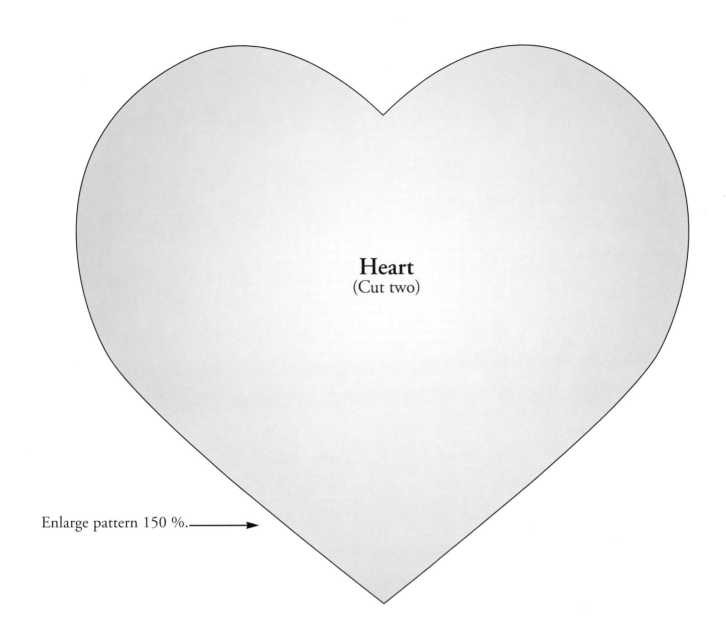

Heart
(Cut two)

Enlarge pattern 150 %.

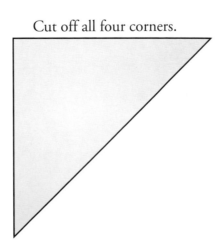

Cut off all four corners.

Watering Can Charm

Cat Charm

Diagram reduced 75 %.

96

Symbol	Stitch	Color	Amt.	Size	Type
Lace	Gathering	White	40"	½"	
	Lazy Daisy	Pale Pink	130" in all	4mm	Silk
	Pistol Stitch	Pale Pink	see above	4mm	Silk
	Ribbon Stitch	Bright Green	42"	4mm	Silk
	Ribbon Stitch	Pale Green	62"	4mm	Silk
	Zigzag Flowers	Dark Pink/Pale Pink	35"	1"	Wired
	Fuchsia	Peach/Bright Pink	15"	2"	Wired
	Buds	Lavender Blue	4½"	⅝"	Wired
	Ribbon Stitch	Bright Green	45"	7mm	Silk
	Coleus Leaf	Peach/Green	10"	⅝"	Wired
	Lazy Daisy	Olive Green	36" in all	7mm	Silk
	Cascade Bow	Olive Green	see above	7mm	Silk
	French knot in bow	Pale Pink	see above	4mm	Silk

Charms
Cat
Watering Can

Robin in the Roses

1

Stitched on platinum Belfast linen 32 over 2 threads, the finished design size is 4⅛" x 3¼". The fabric was cut 8" x 8".

Fabrics	Design Sizes
Aida 11	6" x 4¾"
Aida 14	4¾" x 3¾"
Aida 18	3⅝" x 2⅞"
Hardanger 22	3" x 2⅜"

Stitch Count: 66 x 52

2

Stitched on light mocha Cashel linen 28 over 2 threads, the finished design size is 8½" x 4¼". The fabric was cut 14" x 12".

Fabrics	Design Sizes
Aida 11	10⅞" x 5¾"
Aida 14	8½" x 4¼"
Aida 18	6⅝" x 3½"
Hardanger 22	5⅜" x 2⅞"

Stitch Count: 119 x 63

3

Stitched on platinum Belfast linen 32 over 2 threads, the finished design size is 7½" x 5¾". The fabric was cut 12" x 8".

Fabrics	Design Sizes
Aida 11	11" x 8¼"
Aida 14	8⅝" x 6½"
Aida 18	6¾" x 5"
Hardanger 22	5½" x 4⅛"

Stitch Count: 121 x 91

4

Stitched on antique white Belfast linen 32 over 2 threads, the finished design size is 8¾" x 7". The fabric was cut 15" x 13".

Fabrics	Design Sizes
Aida 11	12⅞" x 10⅛"
Aida 14	10⅛" x 7⅞"
Aida 18	7⅞" x 6⅛"
Hardanger 22	6⅜" x 5"

Stitch Count: 141 x 111

Anchor			DMC (used for sample)

Step 1: Cross-stitch (2 strands)

Anchor			DMC (used for sample)
1	·	◿	White
301	+	◿	744 Yellow-pale
366	−	◿	951 Peach Pecan-lt.
881	✓		945 Peach Beige
914	⸫	◿	3064 Pecan-lt.
5975	◲	◿	356 Terra Cotta-med.
341	▲	◿	3777 Terra Cotta-vy. dk.
49	∴	◿	963 Wild Rose-vy. lt.
25	✛	◿	3326 Rose-lt.
69	◑		3687 Mauve
44	■		814 Garnet-dk.
869	○	◿	3743 Antique Violet-vy. lt.
35	✦		3801 Christmas Red-lt.
47	♣		321 Christmas Red
20	⸙		498 Christmas Red-dk.
265	△	◿	3348 Yellow Green-lt.
266	⤙	◿	3347 Yellow Green-med.
257	★	◿	3346 Hunter Green
269	✳		936 Avocado Green-vy. dk.
862	●		934 Black Avocado Green
878	✱		501 Blue Green-dk.
905	◣	◿	3781 Mocha Brown-dk.
382	♥	◿	3371 Black Brown

Step 2: Backstitch (1 strand)

Anchor		DMC (used for sample)
27	⌐	899 Rose-med. (small flowers)
44	⌐	814 Garnet-dk. (roses)
341	⌐	3777 Terra Cotta-vy. dk. (lettering)
382	⌐	3371 Black Brown (robin)

Stage 1

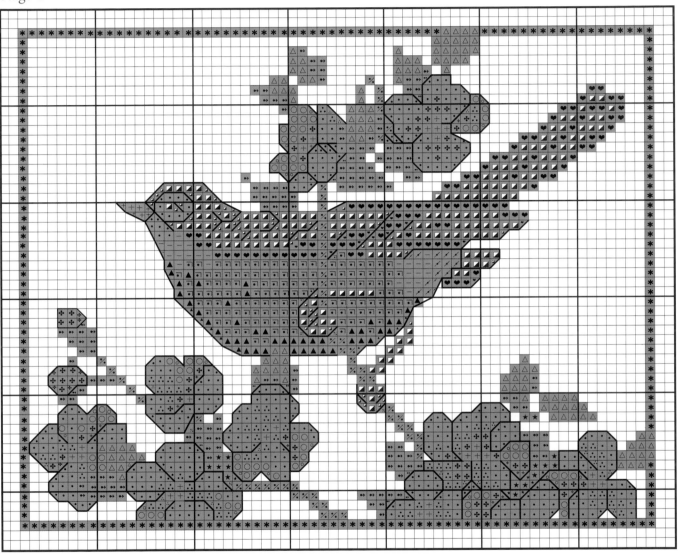

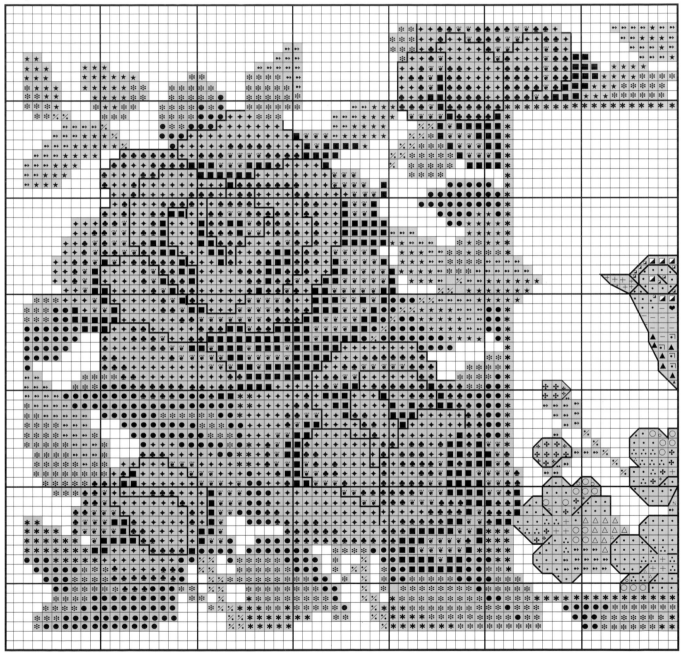

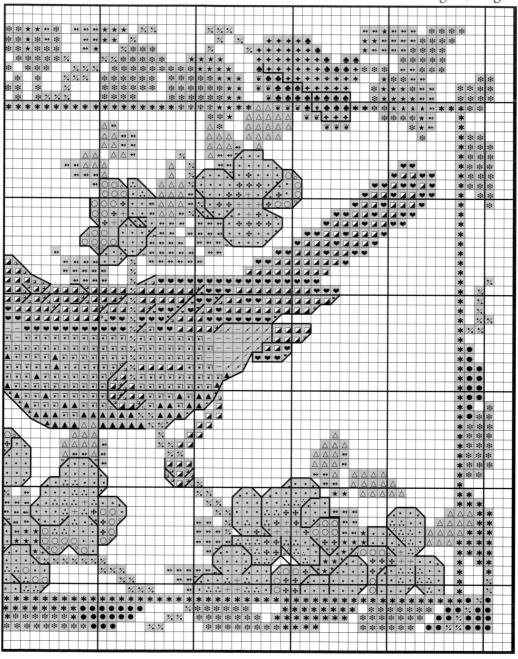

Stages 3 and 4, Top Left

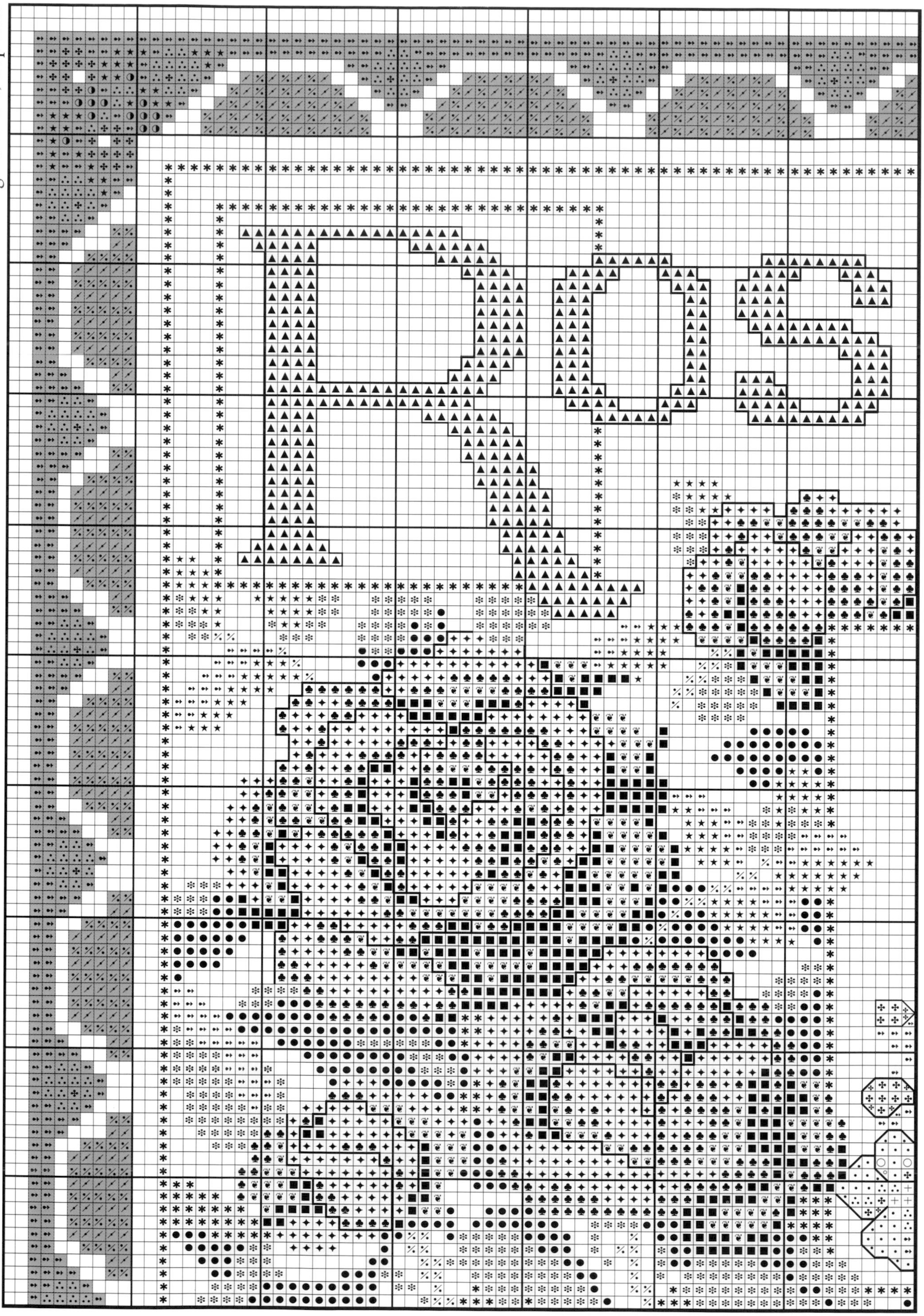

Stages 3 and 4, Top Center

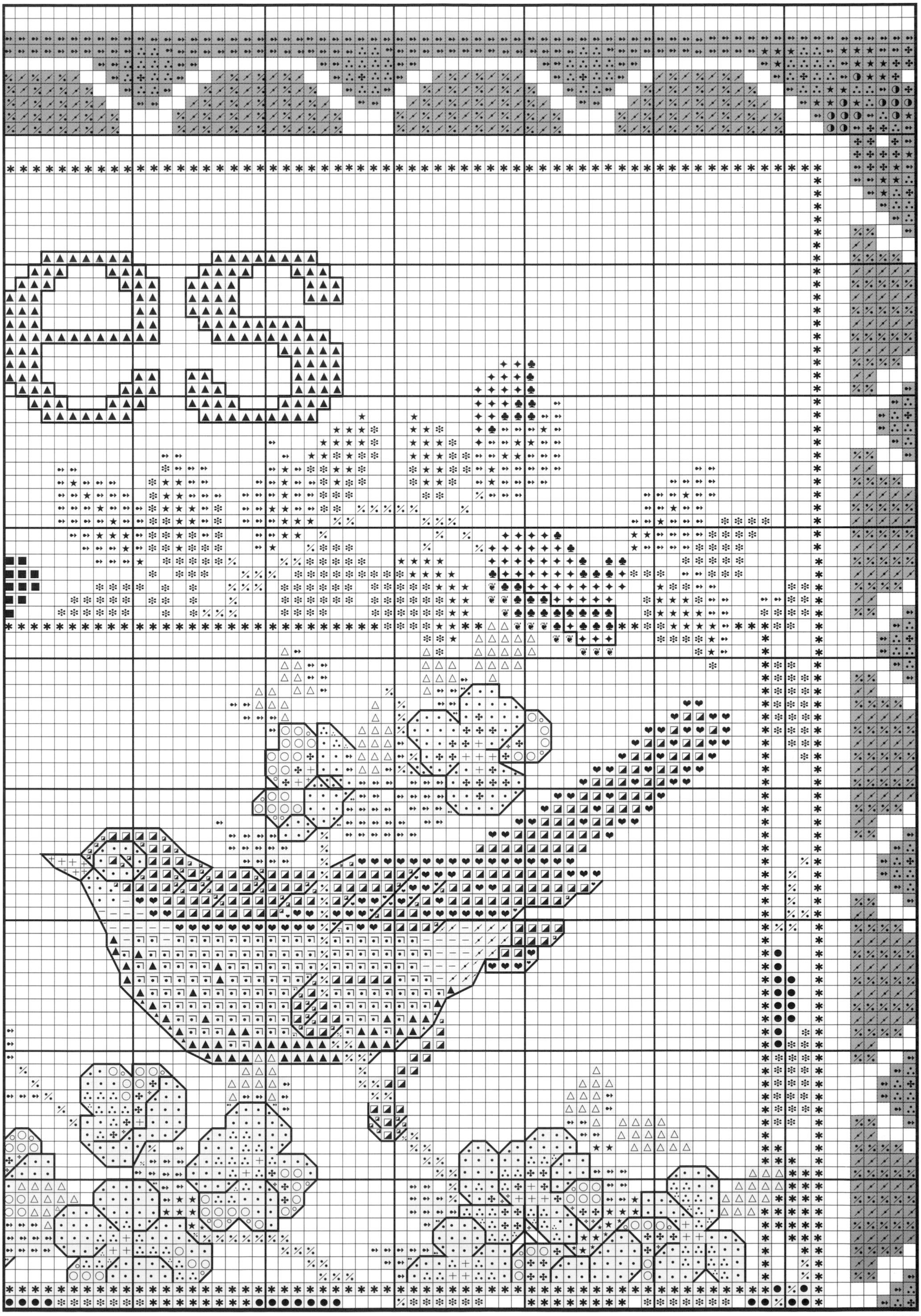

Stages 3 and 4, Top Right

Stages 3 and 4, Bottom Left

Stages 3 and 4, Bottom Right

1-Sachet
Materials

Completed cross-stitch
12½" x 5½" piece of dark
  green wool; matching
  thread
20" of lace trim; matching
  thread
Potpourri
Embellishments (ribbons,
  charms)

Directions

1

Cut wool in half so that you
have two 6¼" x 5½" pieces.
Place together and sew a ¼"
seam around edges, leaving an
opening to turn. Clip corners,
turn and press.

2

Trim cross-stitch to ½" of last
row of stitching. Turn edges
under ¼" and press. Center
cross-stitch on wool and
machine-stitch through all
thicknesses, leaving same side
open.

3

Pin lace trim in place around
edge of stitched piece.
Hand-sew.

4

Stuff both openings with
potpourri. Machine-stitch top
opening closed and whipstitch
wool closed.

5

Embellish with silk ribbons and
charms.

3-Pillow
Materials

Completed cross-stitch
12" x 10" dark green moiré for
  pillow back; matching
  thread
1½ yards matching piping
1½ yards matching ruffle
Stuffing

Directions

1

Trim cross-stitch 1½" from
stitching. Cut pillow back the
same size.

2

Pin piping around pillow front
½" in from edge. Stitch in
place. Pin ruffle, with right side
facing pillow front, next to
outside edge of piping. Stitch
in place.

3

Place pillow back face down on
top of ruffles and sew around
edges on outside of piping,
leaving an opening to turn.
Clip corners, turn and stuff
firmly. Whipstitch opening
closed.

Symbol	Stitch	Color	Amt.	Size	Type
	Ribbon Stitch/ Satin Stitch Style	Wine Red	90"	4mm	Silk
	Beading	Rose Metallic	1 package	seed	
	Beading	Brown Metallic	1 package	seed	
	Ribbon Stitch	White	54"	7mm	Silk
	Ribbon Stitch	Pale Pink	18"	4mm	Silk
	Ribbon Stitch	Medium Pink	44" in all	4mm	Silk
	French Knot	Yellow	27"	4mm	Silk
	Lazy Daisy	Light Olive Green	18"	7mm	Silk
	Lazy Daisy	Dark Olive Green	30"	4mm	Silk
	Ribbon Stitch	Pale Green	30"	4mm	Silk
	Twisted ribbons Couched with Beads	Dusty Green Dark Green	38" 38"	7mm 7mm	Silk Silk
	Beads	Dark Green	1 package.	seed	
	Beads	Light Green	1 package.	seed	
	Lazy Daisy	Medium Pink	see above	4mm	Silk
	Ribbon Stitch	Dark Green	30"	4mm	Silk

Continue ribbon and bead borders around sections.

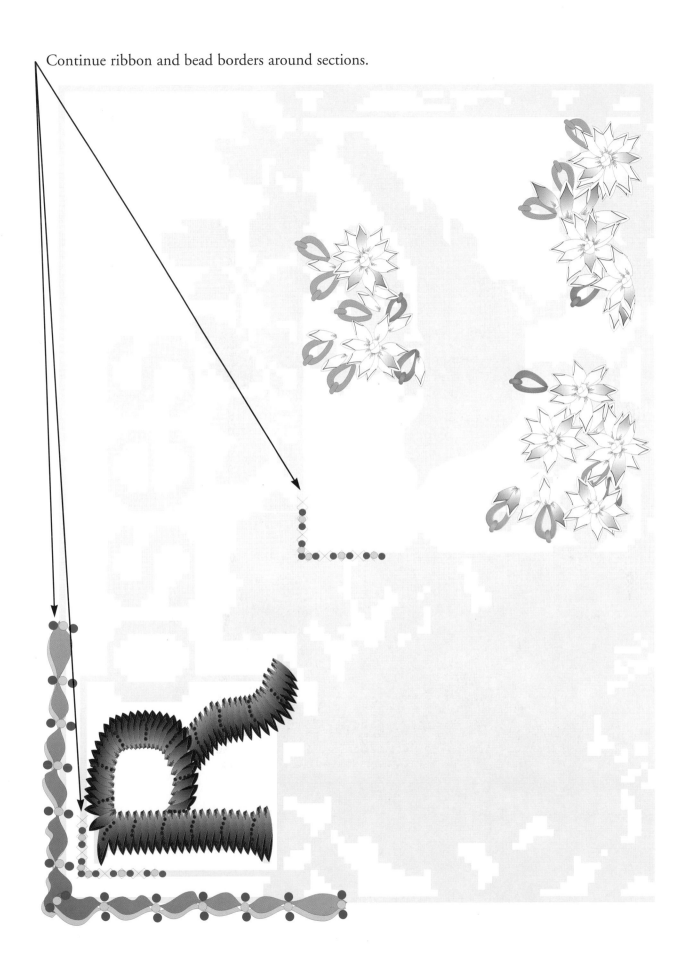

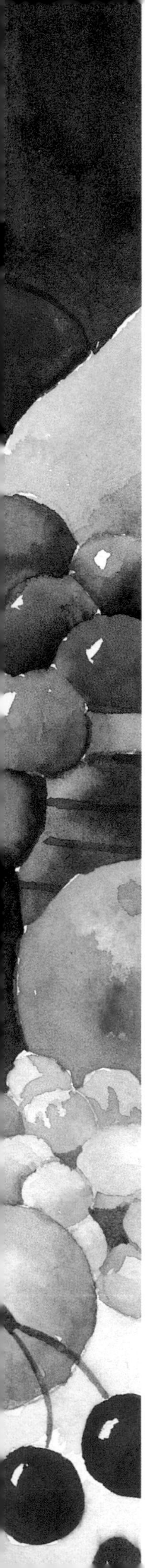

Christmas Feast

1

Stitched on eggshell checkerboard toweling 11 over 1 thread, the finished design size for one repeat is 2⅜" x 1¼". The fabric was a purchased towel.

Fabrics	Design Sizes
Aida 11	2⅜" x 1¼"
Aida 14	1⅞" x 1"
Aida 18	1½" x ¾"
Hardanger 22	1⅛" x ⅝"

Stitch Count: 26 x 14 per repeat

2

Stitched on ash rose Murano linen 30 over 2 threads, the finished design size is 3¼" x 2⅛". The fabric was cut 8" x 8".

Fabrics	Design Sizes
Aida 11	4⅜" x 3"
Aida 14	3⅜" x 2¼"
Aida 18	2⅝" x 1¾"
Hardanger 22	2⅛" x 1½"

Stitch Count: 48 x 32

3

Stitched on light mocha Cashel linen 28 over 2 threads, the finished design size is 9¼" x 2⅞". The fabric was cut 21" x 8".

Fabrics	Design Sizes
Aida 11	11⅝" x 3¾"
Aida 18	7⅛" x 2¼"
Hardanger 22	5⅞" x 1⅞"

Stitch Count: 128 x 41

4

Stitched on twilight blue Belfast linen 32 over 2 threads, the finished design size is 8" x 4¼". The fabric was cut 12" x 8".

Fabrics	Design Sizes
Aida 11	11⅝" x 6⅛"
Aida 14	9⅛" x 4¾"
Aida 18	7⅛" x 3¾"
Hardanger 22	5⅞" x 3"

Stitch Count: 128 x 67

5

Stitched on raw Belfast linen 32 over 2 threads, the finished design size is 8⅜" x 6½". The fabric was cut 17" x 12".

Fabrics	Design Sizes
Aida 11	12⅛" x 9½"
Aida 14	9⅝" x 7⅜"
Aida 18	7½" x 5¾"
Hardanger 22	6⅛" x 4¾"

Stitch Count: 134 x 104

6

Stitched on black Belfast linen 32 over 2 threads, the finished design size is 9⅜" x 7½". The fabric was cut 16" x 14".

Fabrics	Design Sizes
Aida 11	13¾"" x 10⅞"
Aida 14	10¾" x 8⅝"
Aida 18	8⅜" x 6⅝"
Hardanger 22	6⅞" x 5 1/2"

Stitch Count: 150 x 120

Anchor   DMC (used for sample)

Step 1: Cross-stitch (2 strands)

Anchor		DMC	
926	◇		Ecru
301	×	744	Yellow-pale
305		3821	Straw
891	□	676	Old Gold-lt.
373	▼	3045	Yellow Beige-dk.
890	+	3827	Golden Brown-pale
323	F	722	Orange Spice-lt.
326	★	720	Orange Spice-dk.
6	J	3824	Apricot-lt.
35	○	3801	Christmas Red-lt.
13	S	349	Coral-dk.
47	A	321	Christmas Red
20	E	498	Christmas Red-dk.
9		760	Salmon
10	♣	3712	Salmon-med.
69		3803	Mauve-med. dk.
70	B	3685	Mauve-dk.
44		814	Garnet-dk.
101	♥	327	Antique Violet-vy. dk.
978	✳	322	Navy Blue-vy. lt.
941	W	791	Cornflower Blue-vy. dk.
264		772	Pine Green-lt.
257	K	3346	Hunter Green
214	U	368	Pistachio Green-lt.
216	M	367	Pistachio Green-dk.
859		3052	Green-Gray-med.
862		3362	Pine Green-dk.
879	●	500	Blue Green-vy. dk.
933	▽	543	Beige Brown-ultra vy. lt.
376		842	Beige Brown-vy. lt.
379	✳	840	Beige Brown-med.
363	N	436	Tan
370	▲	434	Brown-lt.
308	−	976	Golden Brown-med.
884	G	3826	Golden Brown
355	■	975	Golden Brown-dk.
397	Z	762	Pearl Gray-vy. lt.
399	◑	451	Shell Gray-dk.
301	△	744	Yellow-pale
336		3825	Pumpkin-pale
305	◒	3821	Straw
336		3825	Pumpkin-pale
336	✚	3825	Pumpkin-pale
11		351	Coral
72		902	Garnet-vy.dk.
101		327	Antique Violet-vy. dk.

Anchor		DMC	
101	H	327	Antique Violet-vy. dk.
941		791	Cornflower Blue-vy. dk.
300	·	745	Yellow-lt. pale
264		772	Pine Green-lt.
264	R	772	Pine Green-lt.
214		368	Pistachio Green-lt.
376	✦	842	Beige Brown-vy. lt.
378		841	Beige Brown-lt.

Step 2: Backstitch (1 strand)

Anchor		DMC	
326		720	Orange Spice-dk. (orange)
10		3712	Salmon-med. (flowers in teapot, peaches)
978		322	Navy Blue-vy. lt. (bowl)
216		367	Pistachio Green-dk. (bowl)
379		840	Beige Brown-med. (teapot)
370		434	Brown-lt. (basket)
355		975	Golden Brown-dk. (pineapple)
127		939	Navy Blue-vy. dk. (purple grapes)

Step 3: French knot (1 strand)

Anchor		DMC	
403	●	310	Black

Stage 1, Strawberries

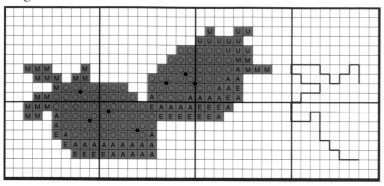

Stage 2 and 3, Left

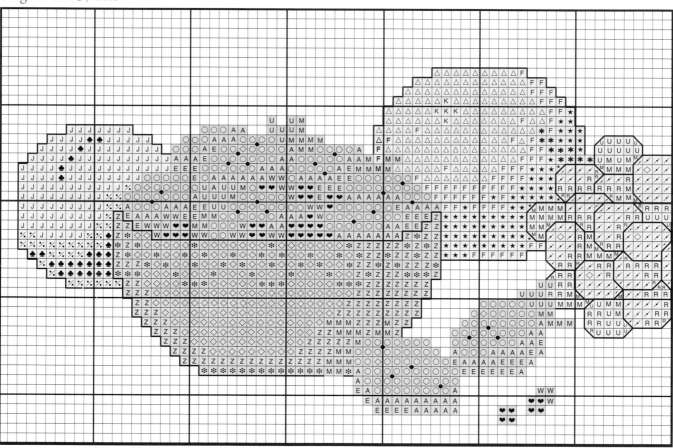

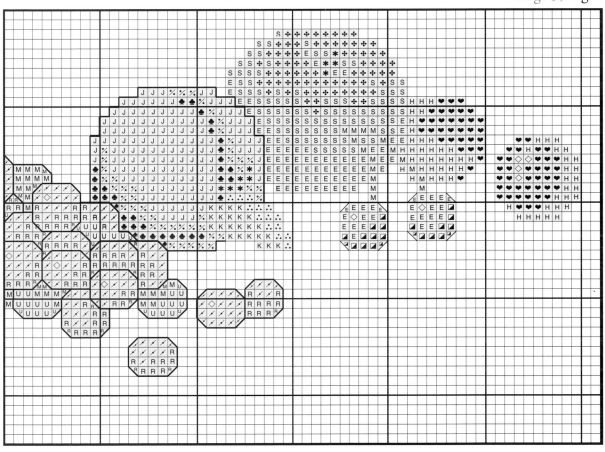

Stages 4, 5, and 6, Top Left

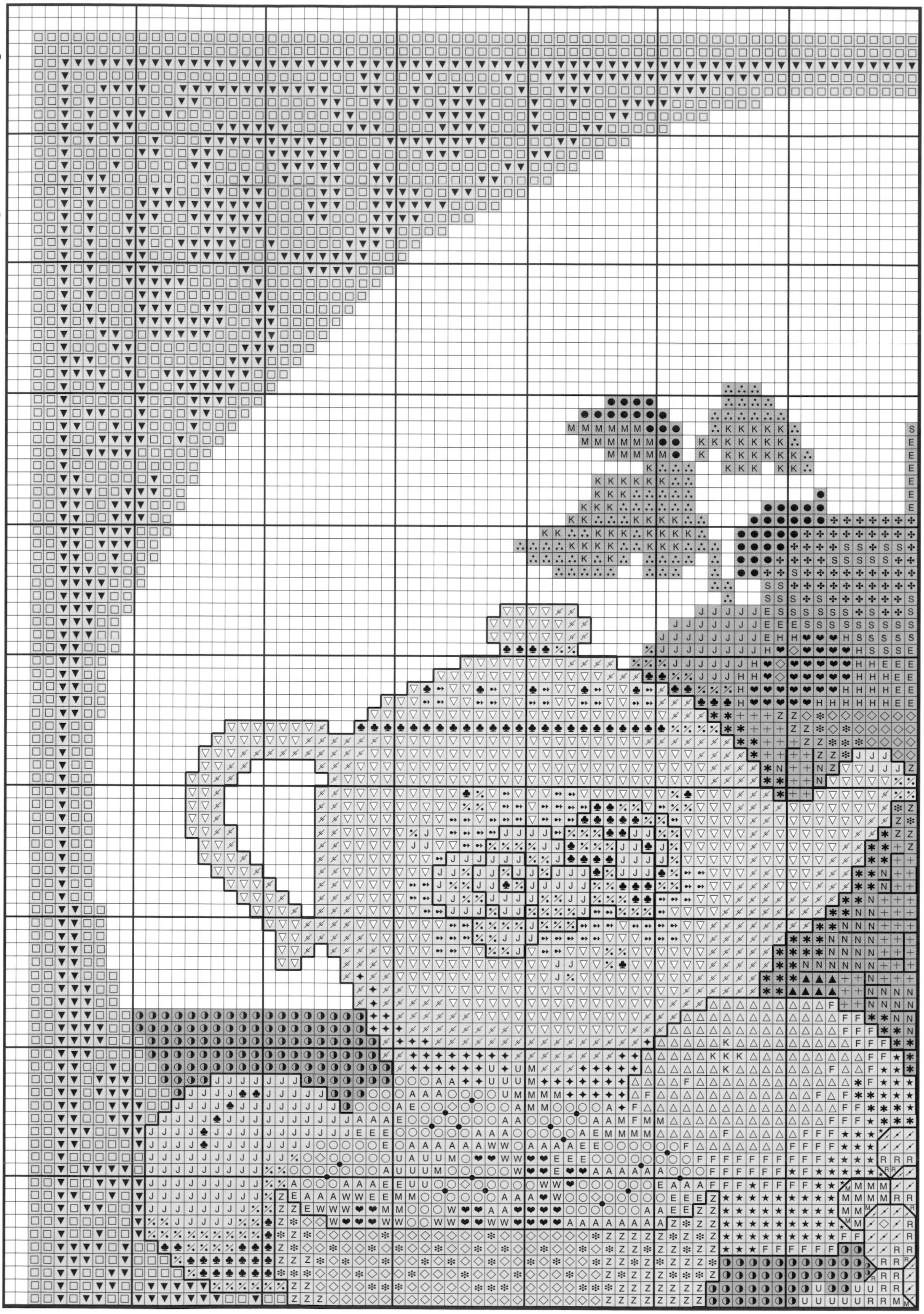

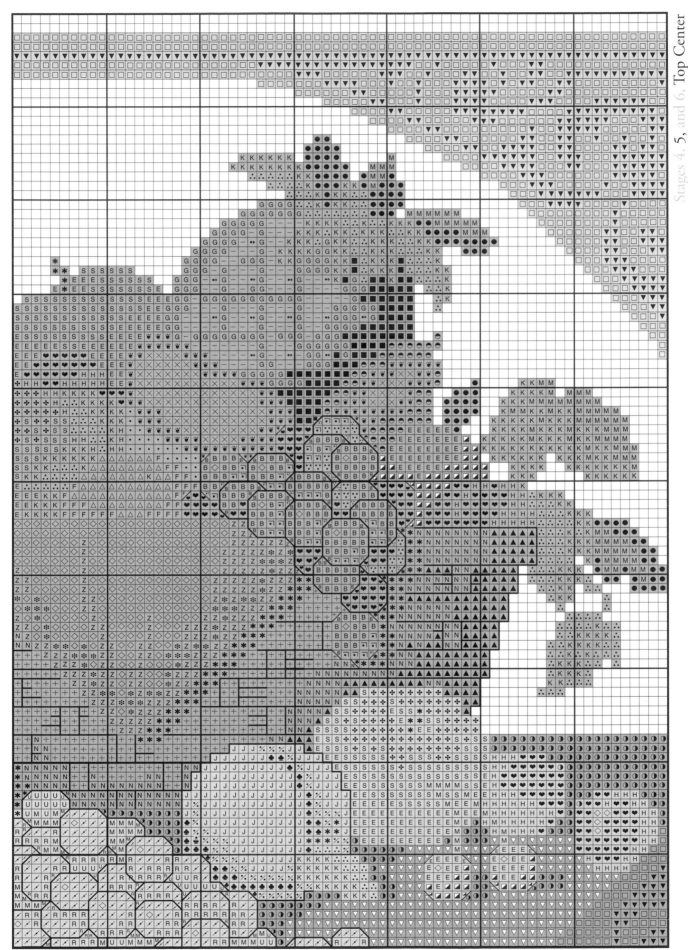

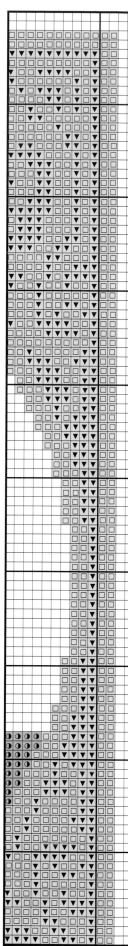

from **On Going Home for Christmas**

Are you going home for Christmas? Have you
written you'll be there?
Going home to kiss the mother and to show her
that you care?
Going home to greet the father in a way to make
him glad?
If you're not I hope there'll never come a time
you'll wish you had.
Just sit down and write a letter–it will make their
heartstrings hum
With a tune of perfect gladness–if you'll tell them
that you'll come.

Edgar Guest

Stages 4, 5, and 6, **Bottom Left**

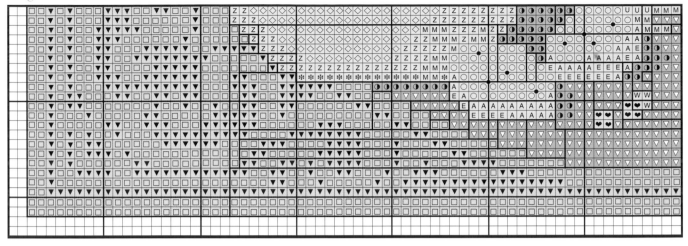

Stages 4, 5, and 6, **Bottom Center**

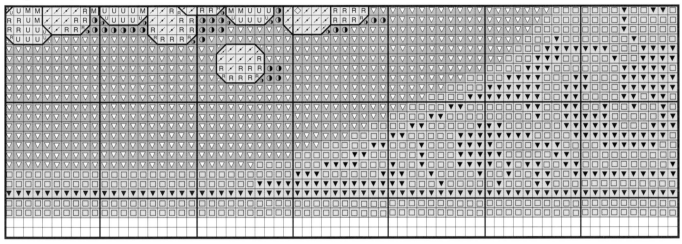

Stages 4, 5, and 6, **Bottom Right**

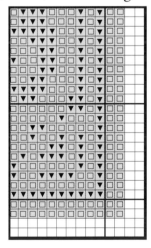

1-Towel
Materials

Completed cross-stitch on
  white
  toweling
1½ yards each green, blue, and
  purple 4mm silk ribbon
9 Crewel needle

Directions

Stitch borders on top and
bottom of cross-stitch with silk
ribbon, following general
ribbon work instructions.
Green border: extended
japanese ribbon stitch; blue
border: straight stitch; purple
border: coral stitch.

2-Hot Pad
Materials

Completed cross-stitch
  trimmed to 6" square
Contrasting fabric 8½" square;
  matching thread
Two 6" squares of fleece
1½ yards of 4mm matching
  silk ribbon

Directions

1

Layer fabrics as follows:
fabric, two layers of fleece,
and stitched piece. Starting at
the bottom edge, roll hem up
over edges and hand-sew all
around hot pad.

2

Cut a strip of fabric 4" x 2".
Fold in half lengthwise and
press. Fold edges in to the
center. Press and stitch. This is
your loop. Sew to top back of
hot pad.

3

Blanket-stitch around edges
with ribbon if desired.

3-Canister
Materials

Completed cross-stitch
6" wooden shaker-style canister
  with lid
Wood knob
Black acrylic paint
Dark walnut stain
Satin finish spray
Tacky glue
Fray preventative
Paintbrushes
Drill

Directions

1

Trim cross-stitch piece to fit
around canister. Apply fray
preventative to raw edges and
let dry.

2

Using tacky glue, run a bead
down back seam of box. Wrap
fabric around canister, turning
edge under when you come
back to seam. Pull snugly. Place
a bead of glue around top and
bottom edges of canister. Smear
with finger to seal fabric to
canister. Let dry.

3

Stain top of lid with dark
walnut stain and paint sides of
lid with black paint. Let dry
and then apply satin finish
spray.

4

Drill hole in center of lid and
attach brass knob hardware.

5-Tea Cozy
Materials

Completed cross-stitch
　　trimmed to 15" x 10"
½ yard fabric for back;
　　matching thread
½ yard fleece
½ yard ⅛"-wide piping
Tassel

Directions

1

Place tea cozy pattern over cross-stitch piece with cross-stitch centered horizontally and with bottom edge 2" below cross-stitch; cut. Cut one tea cozy pattern from unstitched fabric, two from print fabric and two from fleece. From print fabric, cut 1"-wide bias strips, piecing as needed to equal 29". Place the cording in the center of the wrong side of the bias strip and fold the fabric over it. Using a zipper foot, stitch close to the cording through both layers of fabric. Trim the seam allowance ¼" from the stitching line.

2

To make cozy, stitch piping on curved edge of cross-stitch piece with right sides facing and raw edges aligned. Baste one fleece tea cozy shape to wrong side of each tea cozy. Stitch cozies with right sides facing, sewing on stitching line of piping and leaving straight edge open. Clip curves. Trim fleece from seam allowance; turn.

3

To make lining, stitch curved edge of print cozies with right sides facing and raw edges aligned, leaving straight edge open and an opening in curved edge for turning. Slide lining over cozy, right sides facing and raw edges aligned; stitch straight edge. Turn. Slip-stitch opening closed. Fold lining inside cozy. Tack tassel to top of cozy.

Place on fold.

Tea Cozy Pattern
1 square = 1"
Cut 6

Symbol	Stitch	Color	Amt.	Size	Type
Lace	Gathering	Ivory	15"	⅜"	
	Grape	Pink/Purple	4½"	1½"	Wired
	Grape	Purple/Black	10½"	1½"	Wired
	Grape	Pink/Black	7½"	1½"	Wired
	Grape	Yellow/Green	7½"	¾"	Wired
	Grape	Peach/Green	24"	1¼"	Wired
	Grape	Green/Black	7½"	1½"	Wired
	Whipped Running Stitch	Dark Peach Medium Peach	12" 12"	4mm 4mm	Silk Silk
	Touch of Class Rose	Dark, Medium, and Pale Peach	24" in all	4mm	Silk
	Ribbon Stitch	Dark, Medium, and Pale Peach	see above	4mm	Silk
	Ribbon Stitch	Olive Green	30" in all	4mm	Silk
	Lazy Daisy	Olive Green	30" see above	4mm	Silk

Ribbon Embroidery General Instructions

Preparation

Ribbon: To complete each project, you will need to purchase the ribbons listed in the stitch guide next to the stitch diagram. Before you begin, you should press the silk ribbon using low heat to remove any creases. Cut the ribbon into 18" lengths to reduce the chance of the silk ribbon fraying while stitching. Because of the delicate nature of silk ribbon, it can easily become worn, losing some of its body. If this happens, lightly moisten the silk ribbon and it will self-restore. Also, it is important to note that, because silk is a natural fiber, there may be slight color hue differences between strands. Have no fear! The elegance of silk ribbon embroidery is accentuated by this subtle shading.

Needles: As a rule of thumb, the barrel of the needle must create a hole large enough for the ribbon to go through. If the ribbon does not pull through the fabric easily enough, it is because a larger needle is needed. Also, the eye of the needle must be large enough for the ribbon to lay flat when threaded.

Diagrams: The diagrams in this book are shaded to look like the ribbon used in the book. However, the stitches themselves should be much looser than they appear in the diagrams. All stitching should be full and loose enough to cover the cross-stitched area. Use the diagrams for placement and a general idea of what the stitching should look like. Refer to the photos to get an even clearer idea of how the ribbon work should look.

The Method of Ribbon Embroidery

Threading and Locking Ribbon: Pull about 3" of ribbon through the eye of the needle. (1) Pierce the 3" portion of ribbon about ½" from the end. (2) Pull back on the opposite end until it locks securely around the eye of the needle; see diagram.

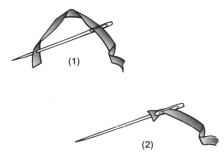

Knotting the End of the Ribbon: To create a soft knot prior to stitching, drape the silk ribbon in a circular manner to position the end of the silk ribbon perpendicular to the tip of the needle. (1) Pierce the end of the silk ribbon with the needle, sliding the needle through the silk ribbon as if to make a short basting stitch. (2) Pull the needle and silk ribbon through the stitched portion to form a knot at the ribbon end; see diagram.

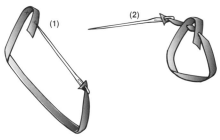

Manipulating the Silk Ribbon: One of the most important aspects of silk ribbon embroidery is manipulation of the silk ribbon. For most stitches, the silk ribbon must be kept flat, smooth and loose. You must use your thumb and the needle to manipulate the ribbon as you stitch or the ribbon may curl and fold, affecting the appearance of your picture; see diagram on page 133. Untwist the ribbon during each stitch and use the needle to lift and straighten the ribbon. Pull the ribbon gently to allow the stitches to lie softly on top of the fabric. Exact stitch placement is not critical, but you will want to make sure that any placement marks are covered by ribbon stitches. You may add a few extra petals or leaves by using any leftover ribbon. There are no mistakes, only variations. Be creative with your stitching.

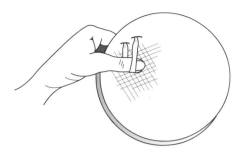

To End Stitching: Secure your stitches in place for each flower or small area before beginning a new area. Do not drag the ribbon from one area to another. Tie a slip knot on the wrong side of your needlework to secure the stitch in place and end ribbon.

Caring for Your Projects: It is recommended to spot-clean only, but due to the need to continually clean clothing, hand-wash with mild dishwashing detergent. If needed, carefully press around embroidered design.

S*titch* G*uide*

Beading Stitch

Using one strand of floss, come up through fabric. Slide the beads on the needle and push the needle back down through fabric. Knot off each set of beads.

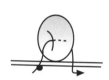

Buds

To make one-petaled buds, cut a 2¾" length of ribbon. Stitch a gathering stitch as shown in diagram. Pull thread tightly to gather; secure thread.

2¾"

Geranium Buds

Cut a 1½" length of ribbon for each bud. Fold ribbon in half lengthwise; press. Fold ribbon as shown in diagrams (A) and (B) and secure with stitches. Stitch a gathering stitch along the remaining length of ribbon

(C). Pull thread tightly to gather; secure thread.
(D) Hand-stitch each bud in place, tucking under raw edges of ribbon where possible. Cover raw edges of buds with ribbon stitches.

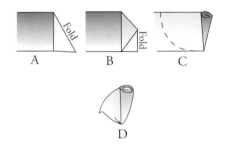

Butterfly

Fold the lighter, ombré ribbon over ⅜"; then mark and stitch as shown in diagram on page 134. Pull thread to gather as

tightly as possible. Secure thread. Join wings, hiding raw edges. Fold the darker ombré ribbon in half, matching long

edges. Gather-stitch as shown in diagram on page 134. Pull thread as tight as possible to gather. Secure thread. Join wings, hiding raw edges. Place and stitch bottom wings. Place and stitch top wings. Shape. Ribbon-stitch the butterfly center for body. Add pistol stitches for antennas.

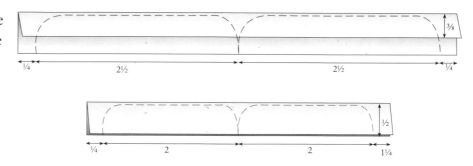

Cascading Stitch

The Cascading Stitch can be done starting with a bow or just using ribbon to "cascade" streamers through design. If starting with a bow, tie bow leaving streamers long enough to work "cascade" through design. Thread streamer on needle, stitch down through fabric where bow placement is desired and come back up at start of "cascade" effect. This will hold the bow in place.
(1) Come up at A and go down at B. Come back up at C, allowing ribbon to twist and lay loosely on the fabric.

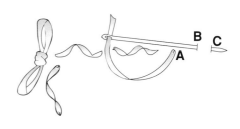

Coleus Leaf

Cut a 5" length of ⅝" wired ribbon. Fold ribbon in half, matching short ends. Turn folded ribbon corners up ⅛" from top edge. Following dashed line, stitch with gathering stitches. Pull thread so that ribbon measures 1½" long. Secure thread. Open and shape leaf. Tack leaf to fabric, hiding raw edge.

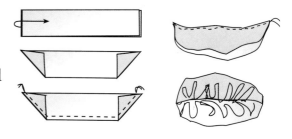

French Knot

(1) Bring needle up through fabric; smoothly wrap ribbon once around needle.
(2) Hold ribbon securely off to one side and push needle down through fabric next to starting point.
(3) Completed French knots. (Number in parentheses in stitch guides indicates how many times to wrap the ribbon around the needle.)

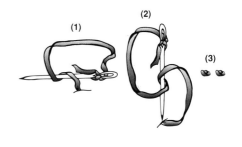

Fuchsias

(1) Cut three 4½" lengths of ribbon. Fold in half with short ends together. Crease ribbon on fold to mark center. Fold one end of ribbon to center, overlapping ¼". Fold remaining end down ¼". Fold to meet center, pin.

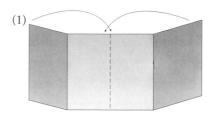

(2) Draw diamond with disappearing pen. (3) Gather diamond, pull tight and tie off. Shape flower. Stitch in place. Use pistil stitches for stamens.

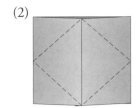
(2)

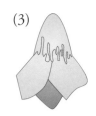
(3)

Grapes

Cut as many 1½" lengths of ribbon as needed. Gather-stitch around each piece of ribbon. Pull thread to gather and secure thread. You will have a "yo-yo." At the outer edge of each "yo-yo," gather and self-stuff with raw edges of ribbon. Secure thread. Stitch all grapes with the quantity required for each shade of ribbon. Stitch or glue grapes in place, having two or three for each cluster laying on top of the bottom layer of grapes.

Jonquil Leaves

Cut ½" wired ribbon into eight 3 ¼" lengths. Fold lengths as in diagram. Make a gathering stitch at bottom edge of folded ribbon with a ¼" seam allowance. Wrap the thread around the ribbon twice; secure. Stitch leaves in place.

Lazy Daisy

(1) Bring the needle up at A. Keep the ribbon flat, untwisted and full. Put the needle down through fabric at B and up through at C, keeping the ribbon under the needle to form a loop. Pull the ribbon through, leaving the loop loose and full. To hold the loop in place, go down on other side of ribbon near C, forming a straight stitch over loop. (2) Completed lazy daisy.

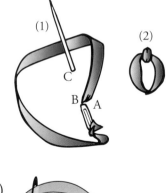
(1)
(2)

Bullion Lazy Daisy

Complete as above, but tack with a bullion stitch. (1) To make bullion stitch, bring needle down and up through fabric, but do not pull through. (2) Wrap loose ribbon around needle tip twice. Holding

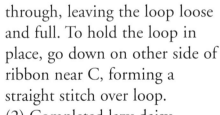
(1)
(2)

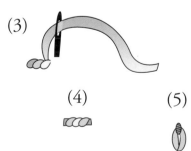
(3)
(4)
(5)

finger over wrapped ribbon, pull needle through ribbon. (3) Insert needle again, pulling to fabric back. (4) Completed Bullion Stitch. (5) Completed Bullion Lazy Daisy.

Pansies

(1) Cut an 8" length of ribbon. Beginning and ending ¼" from ends, mark a 2¼" interval, a 4" interval and a 2¼" interval.

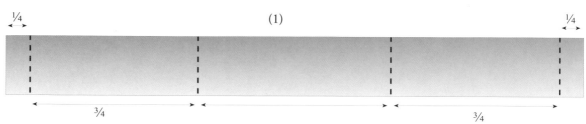

(2) Fold ribbon at marks. Stitch a gathering stitch beginning on outside edge. Pull thread tightly to gather. Stitch raw ends together; secure thread.

(3) For 1"-wide ribbon, fold down one edge ⅜", and then mark and stitch as for above pansies. This creates extra texture and shading.

(4) Stitch a French knot in the center of each pansy.

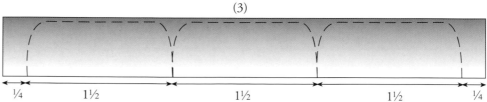

Two and Three-Petaled Pansy Buds

(1) To make two-petaled buds, cut a 3½" length of ribbon. Beginning and ending ¼" from ends, mark 1½" intervals.
(2) Fold ribbon at marks and stitch a gathering stitch.
(3) For three-petaled buds, use 5" lengths of ribbon and mark three 1½" intervals.

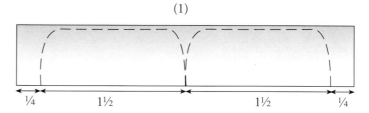

(4) Using 4mm silk ribbon, make straight stitches at bases of pansy buds. Make ribbon stitches onto the body of the buds, forming the calyx.

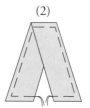

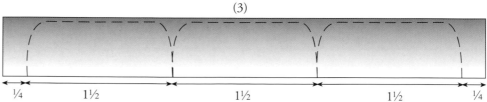

Pistil Stitch

This stitch creates the look of a straight stitch with a French knot on the end.
(1) Bring needle up through fabric at A; smoothly wrap ribbon once (twice for a larger knot on end) around needle.
(2) Hold ribbon securely off to one side and push needle down through fabric at B, the length of the straight stitch portion of the stitch.

(3) Completed Pistil Stitches.

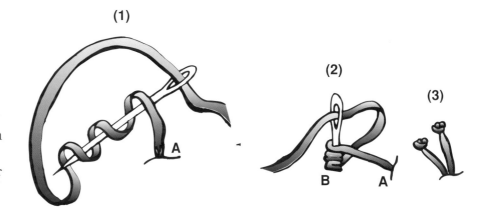

Ribbon Stitch

(1) Come up through fabric at the starting point of stitch. Lay the ribbon flat on the fabric. At the end of the stitch, pierce the ribbon with the needle. Slowly pull the length of the ribbon through to the back, allowing the ends of the ribbon to curl. If the ribbon is pulled too tight, the effect of the stitch will be lost. Vary the petals and leaves by adjusting the length, the tension of the ribbon before piercing, and how loosely or tightly the ribbon is pulled down through itself.
(2) Completed ribbon stitch.

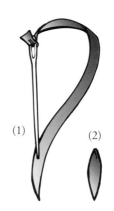

One-Twist Ribbon Stitch

Follow instructions above, adding a twist in the ribbon before pushing the needle back down.

Ribbon Stitch, Satin Style

(1) Satin-style stitches offer a smooth, shiny surface that creates a change of texture. To create this effect, place stitches side by side, so that the underlying fabric does not show through.

(2) When stitching the ribbon stitch, satin-stitch style, you will create a mushroom pleated effect.

Spider Web Rose

(1) Using two strands of matching color or white floss or sewing thread, securely work straight stitches to form five spokes. These are your anchor stitches to create the rose with ribbon.

(2) Bring the piece of ribbon up through the center of the spokes.

(3 & 4) Weave the ribbon over one spoke, and under the next spoke continuing around in one direction (clockwise or counter clockwise), until the spokes are covered. When weaving, keep the ribbon loose and allow it to twist. To end, stitch down through fabric along the last row of petals.

(5) Completed spider web rose.

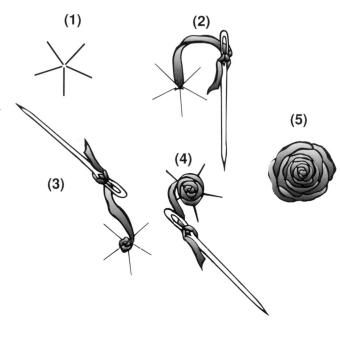

Touch-of-Class Rose

(1) Make bullioned lazy daisy stitches according to stitch diagram to form the center of the rose. Make ribbon stitches and one-twist ribbon stitches around center. (2) Stitch large and small buds in the same fashion, randomly alternating shades of ribbon. (3) Using two shades of ribbon, stitch bullioned lazy daisy stitches and ribbon stitches, forming leaves.

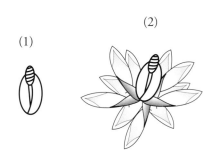

Twisted Ribbon Couched with Beads

(1) Working both ribbons anchor at one corner. Twist as desired, laying ribbons along desired path. (2) Using embroidery floss, make a short tight straight stitch across the ribbon base to "couch" the straight stitch. Place five beads on the needle. (See beading instructions.) Come up at C on one side of the ribbons. Go down at D on the opposite side of the ribbons. The tight, short stitch across the ribbons will cause the ribbons to gather and pucker. The straight stitch base is tacked at varying intervals.

(3) Completed twisted beaded couching stitch.

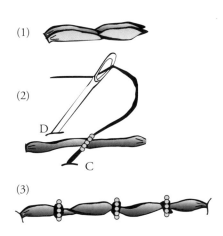

Whipped Running Stitch

(1) Complete the running stitches first. Come up at A and go down at B. Come up at C, allowing an unstitched space between stitches. Continue with next stitch in the same manner as A-B.

(2) To whip the running stitch, go under the first running stitch from A to B. (Be careful not to pierce the fabric or catch the running stitch.) Come up on the other side of the stitch. Keeping the ribbon flat, wrap the ribbon over the stitch and go under the next running stitch at C. Continue in the same manner. The effect can be varied by how loosely or tightly the ribbon is pulled when whipping.

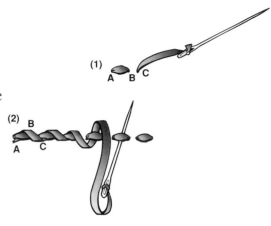

Wild Rose

(1) Bring ribbon to top of fabric. Insert needle back down into fabric right next to starting point, allowing a ¼"-deep loop to remain on fabric's surface. (2) With contrasting ribbon or floss, stitch a French knot in the center of the loop, flattening it to meet the fabric.

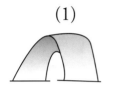

Zigzag Flower

(1) For large flowers, mark the length of ribbon with 13 intervals, as shown, each measuring 1½". Mark opposite side of ribbon with 12 intervals, each 1½", spaced as shown. Gather-stitch the intervals by connecting the marks, as shown. (2) Pull thread to tightly gather. Secure thread. (3) Join ribbon ends at beginning and ending stitch points. Fold dark edge of ribbon inward and connect the centers of each petal, one to the next, until all center petals have been joined. Shape outer petals. Hand-stitch in place; fold half of the flower upwards. For smaller flowers, each interval measures ¾", with 13 on one side and 12 on the other. Stitch as above.

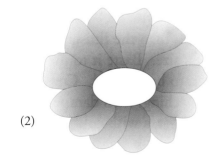

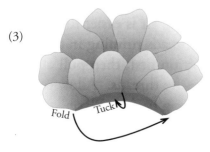

Cross-Stitch General Instructions

Fabrics

Counted cross-stitch is usually worked on even-weave fabrics. These fabrics are manufactured specifically for counted-thread embroidery and are woven with the same number of vertical as horizontal threads per inch. Because the number of threads in the fabric is equal in each direction, each stitch will be the same size. It is the number of threads per inch in even-weave fabrics that determines the size of a finished design. Fabrics used for models are identified in sample informations by color, name, and thread count per inch.

Waste Canvas

Waste canvas is a coarse, fabric-like substance used as a guide for cross-stitching on fabrics other than even weaves. Cut the waste canvas 1" larger on all sides than the finished design size. Baste it to the fabric to be stitched. Complete the stitching; then dampen the stitched area with cold water. Pull the waste canvas thread out one at a time with tweezers. It is easier to pull all the threads running in one direction first, then pull out the opposite threads. Allow the stitching to dry. Place face down on a towel and iron.

Preparing Fabric

Cut fabric at least 3" larger on all sides than finished design size, or cut as indicated in sample information to ensure enough space for project assembly. A 3" margin is the minimum amount of space that allows for comfortably working the edges of the design. To prevent fraying, whipstitch or machine-zigzag along raw edges or apply liquid ravel preventative.

Needles

Needles should slip easily through fabric holes without piercing fabric threads. For fabric with 11 or fewer threads per inch, use needle size 24; for 14 threads per inch, use needle size 24 or 26; for 18 or more threads per inch, use needle size 26. Never leave needle in design area of fabric. It may leave rust or permanent impression on fabric.

Finished Design Size

To determine size of finished design, divide stitch count by number of threads per inch of fabric. When design is stitched over two threads, divide stitch count by half the threads per inch.

Floss

All numbers and color names are cross-referenced between Anchor and DMC brands of floss. Use 18" lengths of floss. For best coverage, separate strands. Dampen with wet sponge. Then put back together the number of strands called for in color code.

Centering the Design

Fold the fabric in half horizontally, then vertically. Place a pin in the fold point to mark the center. Locate the center of the design on the graph by following the vertical and horizontal arrows in the left and bottom margins. Begin stitching all designs at the center point of the graph and the fabric, unless the instructions indicate otherwise.

Graphs

Each symbol represents a different color. Make one stitch for each symbol, referring to the code to verify which stitch to use. Use the small arrows in the margins to find the center of the graph. The stitch count is printed with each graph, listing first the width, then the length, of the design.

Codes

The code indicates the brand of thread used to stitch the model, as well as the cross-reference for using another brand. The steps in the code identify the stitch to be used and the number of floss strands for that stitch. A symbol under a diagonal line indicates a half cross-stitch. Blended threads are represented on the code and graph with a single symbol, but both color names are listed.

Securing the Floss

Insert needle up from the underside of the fabric at starting point. Hold 1" of thread behind the fabric and stitch over it, securing with the first few stitches. To finish thread, turn under four or more stitches on the back of the design. Never knot floss unless working on clothing. Another method of securing floss is the waste knot. Knot floss and insert needle from the right side of the fabric about 1" from design area. Work several stitches over the thread to secure. Cut off the knot later.

Stitching Method

For smooth stitches, use the push-and-pull method. Starting on wrong side of fabric, push needle straight up, pulling floss completely through to right side. Reinsert needle and bring it back straight down, pulling needle and floss completely through to back of fabric. Keep floss flat but do not pull thread tight. For even stitches, tension should be consistent throughout.

Carrying Floss

To carry floss, weave floss under the previously worked stitches on the back. Do not carry thread across any fabric that is not or will not be stitched. Loose threads, especially dark ones, will show through the fabric.

Twisted Floss

If floss is twisted, drop the needle and allow the floss to unwind itself. Floss will cover best when lying flat. Use thread no longer than 18" because it will tend to twist and knot.

Cleaning Completed Work

When stitching is complete, soak it in cold water with a mild soap for five to ten minutes. Rinse well and roll in a towel to remove excess water. Do not wring. Place work face down on a dry towel and iron on warm setting until dry.

Cross-Stitch

Make one cross-stitch for each symbol on chart. Bring needle up at A, down at B, up at C, down at D; see diagram. For rows, stitch across fabric from left to right to make half-crosses and then back to complete stitches.

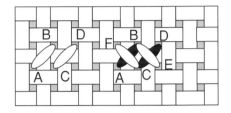

Backstitch

Complete all cross-stitching before working backstitches or other accent stitches. Working from left to right with one strand of floss (unless designated otherwise on code), bring needle and thread up at A, down at B, and up again at C. Continue in this manner.

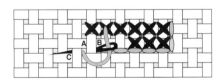

French Knot

Follow directions for ribbon French knot, substituting floss. Floss French knots are generally wrapped around the needle once, unless otherwise indicated in the code.

*M*etric *E*quivalency *C*hart

MM-Millimetres   CM-Centimetres

INCHES TO MILLIMETRES AND CENTIMETRES

INCHES	MM	CM	INCHES	CM	INCHES	CM	
⅛		3	0.3	9	22.9	30	76.2
¼	6	0.6	10	25.4	31	78.7	
½	13	1.3	12	30.5	33	83.8	
⅝	16	1.6	13	33.0	34	86.4	
¾	19	1.9	14	35.6	35	88.9	
⅞	22	2.2	15	38.1	36	91.4	
1	25	2.5	16	40.6	37	94.0	
1¼	32	3.2	17	43.2	38	96.5	
1½	38	3.8	18	45.7	39	99.1	
1¾	44	4.4	19	48.3	40	101.6	
2	51	5.1	20	50.8	41	104.1	
2½	64	6.4	21	53.3	42	106.7	
3	76	7.6	22	55.9	43	109.2	
3½	89	8.9	23	58.4	44	111.8	
4	102	10.2	24	61.0	45	114.3	
4½	114	11.4	25	63.5	46	116.8	
5	127	12.7	26	66.0	47	119.4	
6	152	15.2	27	68.6	48	121.9	
7	178	17.8	28	71.1	49	124.5	
8	203	20.3	29	73.7	50	127.0	

YARDS TO METRES

YARDS	METRES	YARDS	METRES	YARDS	METRES	YARDS	METRES	YARDS	METRES
⅛	0.11	2⅛	1.94	4⅛	3.77	6⅛	5.60	8⅛	7.43
¼	0.23	2¼	2.06	4¼	3.89	6¼	5.72	8¼	7.54
⅜	0.34	2⅜	2.17	4⅜	4.00	6⅜	5.83	8⅜	7.66
½	0.46	2½	2.29	4½	4.11	6½	5.94	8½	7.77
⅝	0.57	2⅝	2.40	4⅝	4.23	6⅝	6.06	8⅝	7.89
¾	0.69	2¾	2.51	4¾	4.34	6¾	6.17	8¾	8.00
⅞	0.80	2⅞	2.63	4⅞	4.46	6⅞	6.29	8⅞	8.12
1	0.91	3	2.74	5	4.57	7	6.40	9	8.23
1⅛	1.03	3⅛	2.86	5⅛	4.69	7⅛	6.52	9⅛	8.34
1¼	1.14	3¼	2.97	5¼	4.80	7¼	6.63	9¼	8.46
1⅜	1.26	3⅜	3.09	5⅜	4.91	7⅜	6.74	9⅜	8.57
1½	1.37	3½	3.20	5½	5.03	7½	6.86	9½	8.69
1⅝	1.49	3⅝	3.31	5⅝	5.14	7⅝	6.97	9⅝	8.80
1¾	1.60	3¾	3.43	5¾	5.26	7¾	7.09	9¾	8.92
1⅞	1.71	3⅞	3.54	5⅞	5.37	7⅞	7.20	9⅞	9.03

Index